Table of Contents

1. **Introduction to Artificial Intelligence**
   - What is AI?
   - Brief History of AI
   - Importance of AI in Today's World

2. **Foundations of AI**
   - Basic Concepts and Terminology
   - Types of AI: Narrow, General, and Superintelligent AI
   - AI vs. Human Intelligence

3. **Key Technologies in AI**
   - Machine Learning
     - Supervised Learning
     - Unsupervised Learning
     - Reinforcement Learning
   - Neural Networks and Deep Learning
   - Natural Language Processing
   - Computer Vision
   - Robotics

4. **AI Tools and Platforms**
   - Popular AI Frameworks and Libraries
   - Cloud-Based AI Services
   - Setting Up Your AI Environment

5. **Applications of AI**

- AI in Healthcare
   - AI in Finance
   - AI in Transportation
   - AI in Entertainment
   - AI in Education

6. **Ethics and Challenges in AI**
   - Ethical Considerations
   - Bias and Fairness in AI
   - Privacy and Security Issues
   - The Future of Work and AI

7. **Getting Started with AI Programming**
   - Introduction to Python for AI
   - Basic AI Programming Exercises
   - Building Your First AI Project

8. **Future Trends in AI**
   - Emerging AI Technologies
   - AI and the Internet of Things (IoT)
   - AI in Augmented and Virtual Reality
   - Predictions for the Future of AI

9. **Resources for Further Learning**
   - Recommended Books and Articles
   - Online Courses and Tutorials
   - AI Communities and Conferences

10. **Conclusion**
    - Recap of Key Points
    - The Future of AI for Beginners
    - Encouragement for Continued Learning

11. **Glossary**
    - Definitions of Key Terms and Concepts

12. **AI Project Workflow**

CHAPTER 1: INTRODUCTION TO ARTIFICIAL INTELLIGENCE

<u>What is AI?</u>

Artificial Intelligence (AI) is the simulation of human intelligence processes by machines, particularly computer systems. These processes include learning (the acquisition of information and rules for using the information), reasoning (using rules to reach approximate or definite conclusions), and self-correction. In more simple terms, AI involves creating systems that can perform tasks that would typically require human intelligence. This can include anything from recognizing speech and making decisions to playing games and interpreting complex data.

<u>Defining AI</u>

To fully grasp AI, it's essential to break down its core components:

- **Learning**: This involves acquiring information and the rules for using that information. AI systems are designed to learn from data, identify patterns, and make decisions with minimal human intervention. The learning process is divided into several types:

  - *Supervised Learning*: The system is trained on a labeled dataset, meaning that each training example is paired with an output label.
  - *Unsupervised Learning*: The system is given data without explicit instructions on what to do with it. The AI must find patterns and relationships within the data.
  - *Reinforcement Learning*: The system learns by receiving rewards or penalties for the actions it performs, thus optimizing its strategy over time.

- **Reasoning**: This involves the process of drawing conclusions from principles and facts. In AI, reasoning systems can apply the rules they've learned to new data to infer new information or make decisions. There are two main types:
  - *Deductive Reasoning*: Drawing specific conclusions from general principles or rules.
  - *Inductive Reasoning*: Making generalizations based on specific instances.

- **Self-Correction**: This ensures that the AI can adjust its algorithms and approaches to improve its accuracy over time. Self-correcting systems can refine their performance by continually learning from new data and feedback.

AI vs. Traditional Programming

Traditional programming involves creating specific instructions for a computer to perform a task, while AI is more about creating systems that can learn to perform tasks on their own. Traditional programming follows a rigid structure where every possible scenario is coded, whereas AI systems use data and algorithms to make decisions without explicit instructions for each scenario.

Brief History of AI

Early Concepts and Theories

The concept of artificial intelligence is not new; it has roots in ancient history. Philosophers and scientists have long imagined the creation of intelligent machines. Here are some key milestones:

- **Antiquity to 19th Century**: Early myths and legends, such as the Greek myth of Pygmalion and Galatea, explore the idea of artificial beings endowed with intelligence.
- **Mid-20th Century**: The formal foundations of AI began to take shape. In 1950, British mathematician and logician Alan Turing published his seminal paper "Computing Machinery and Intelligence," where he introduced the concept of the Turing Test—a method for determining whether a machine can exhibit intelligent behavior indistinguishable from that of a human.

The Birth of AI as a Discipline

AI as a formal discipline started in the mid-20th century with the advent of digital computers. Key events include:

- **Dartmouth Conference (1956)**: Often considered the birthplace of AI as an academic field. Organized by John McCarthy, Marvin Minsky, Nathaniel Rochester, and Claude Shannon, the conference brought together leading researchers to discuss the possibility of creating intelligent machines.
- **Early AI Programs**: The 1950s and 1960s saw the development of the first AI programs. For example, the Logic

Theorist (1955) by Allen Newell and Herbert A. Simon was able to prove mathematical theorems, and ELIZA (1966) by Joseph Weizenbaum could simulate a psychotherapist's conversation.

Evolution Through the Decades

- **1970s to 1980s**: This period saw both optimism and setbacks. While there were significant advancements, such as the development of expert systems, there were also periods of reduced funding and interest, known as "AI winters."

- **1990s to Early 2000s**: AI began to recover, with notable achievements like IBM's Deep Blue defeating chess champion Garry Kasparov in 1997. The rise of the internet provided vast amounts of data, which proved crucial for AI development.

- **2010s to Present**: The modern era of AI is marked by rapid advancements in machine learning, neural networks, and deep learning. AI applications have become integral to everyday life, from voice assistants like Siri and Alexa to sophisticated data analytics tools.

Importance of AI in Today's World

Artificial Intelligence has transformed various aspects of modern life, revolutionizing industries and enhancing daily experiences. Its importance can be highlighted in several key areas:

Enhancing Efficiency and Productivity

AI systems can process vast amounts of data quickly and accurately, leading to increased efficiency and productivity in various sectors. Examples include:

- **Manufacturing**: AI-driven robots and automation systems streamline production processes, reduce errors, and improve quality control.

- **Healthcare**: AI assists in diagnosing diseases, predicting patient outcomes, and personalizing treatment plans, significantly improving healthcare delivery.

Driving Innovation and New Technologies

AI is a catalyst for innovation, leading to the development of new technologies and applications:

- **Autonomous Vehicles**: AI powers self-driving cars, enhancing transportation safety and efficiency.

- **Smart Cities**: AI helps manage urban infrastructure, optimize traffic flow, and improve public services, contributing to sustainable urban development.

Enhancing Decision-Making

AI provides valuable insights and supports decision-making processes across various domains:

- **Business**: AI-driven analytics help companies make data-informed decisions, optimize operations, and understand market trends.

- **Finance**: AI algorithms detect fraudulent activities, manage risks, and assist in investment strategies.

Improving Quality of Life

AI applications enhance everyday life, providing convenience, entertainment, and improved services:

- **Personal Assistants**: AI-powered virtual assistants like Google Assistant and Amazon Alexa make daily tasks easier by responding to voice commands, setting reminders, and controlling smart home devices.
- **Entertainment**: AI enhances user experiences in gaming, streaming services, and personalized content recommendations.

The Future of AI

The potential of AI continues to grow, promising even more significant advancements and challenges. Key areas of future development include:

Human-AI Collaboration

Future AI systems are expected to work alongside humans, complementing human skills and enhancing productivity. This collaboration can lead to innovative solutions and improved problem-solving capabilities.

Ethical and Responsible AI

As AI becomes more integrated into society, ethical considerations will become increasingly important. Ensuring fairness, transparency, and accountability in AI systems will be crucial to addressing issues like bias, privacy, and the impact on employment.

Expanding AI Applications

AI's applications will continue to expand into new domains, including:

- **Healthcare**: AI will play a more significant role in personalized medicine, drug discovery, and managing healthcare systems.
- **Education**: AI-driven tools will provide personalized learning experiences, helping educators address diverse student needs and improve educational outcomes.
- **Environmental Sustainability**: AI can help address environmental challenges by optimizing resource use, monitoring ecosystems, and supporting sustainable practices.

AI and the Global Economy

AI is poised to have a substantial impact on the global economy, influencing job markets, industry structures, and economic growth. Policymakers and businesses will need to adapt to these changes to harness AI's benefits while mitigating potential risks.

Summary

In this chapter, we have introduced the basic concepts and importance of Artificial Intelligence, its historical development, and its transformative impact on various aspects of modern life. As we delve deeper into subsequent chapters, we will explore the foundational technologies, applications, and ethical considerations surrounding AI, providing a comprehensive guide for beginners to understand and engage with this fascinating field.

CHAPTER 2: FOUNDATIONS OF AI

Basic Concepts and Terminology

To understand AI deeply, it's essential to grasp the basic concepts and terminology. This section covers the fundamental terms and ideas that form the foundation of artificial intelligence.

Intelligence

Intelligence is the ability to learn, understand, and apply knowledge to solve problems and adapt to new situations. In AI, intelligence is the capability of machines to mimic these cognitive functions.

Agent

An agent is an entity that perceives its environment through sensors and acts upon that environment through actuators. Agents can be anything from simple software programs to complex robots.

Environment

The environment is everything external to the agent that it interacts with. It can be static or dynamic, discrete or continuous, fully observable or partially observable.

State

The state is a representation of the status of an agent or the environment at a given time. States can be fully observable or partially observable, and they can be deterministic or stochastic.

Action

An action is any move taken by an agent to achieve a specific goal. Actions can be simple, like moving left or right, or complex, like diagnosing a medical condition.

Reward

A reward is feedback received by an agent after performing an action. Rewards can be positive or negative and are used in reinforcement learning to guide the agent's behavior.

Policy

A policy is a strategy used by an agent to decide which actions to take in various situations. In reinforcement learning, policies are learned through interaction with the environment.

Algorithm

An algorithm is a step-by-step procedure used for calculations and data processing. AI algorithms are used to solve problems and make decisions.

Model

A model is an abstract representation of a system that can predict outcomes based on input data. In machine learning, models are trained on data to make predictions or decisions.

Supervised Learning

Supervised learning is a type of machine learning where the model is trained on labeled data. The goal is to learn a mapping from inputs to outputs.

Unsupervised Learning

Unsupervised learning is a type of machine learning where the model is trained on unlabeled data. The goal is to find hidden patterns or structures in the data.

Reinforcement Learning

Reinforcement learning is a type of machine learning where an agent learns by interacting with its environment and receiving rewards or penalties for its actions.

Neural Networks

Neural networks are a series of algorithms that attempt to recognize underlying relationships in a set of data through a process that mimics the way the human brain operates.

Deep Learning

Deep learning is a subset of machine learning that involves neural networks with many layers (deep neural networks). It is used for more complex tasks like image and speech recognition.

Types of AI: Narrow, General, and Superintelligent AI

AI can be categorized into three types based on its capabilities and scope: Narrow AI, General AI, and Superintelligent AI.

Narrow AI

Narrow AI, also known as weak AI, is designed to perform a specific task or a narrow range of tasks. These systems operate under a limited set of constraints and predefined functions.

Characteristics of Narrow AI

- **Task-Specific**: Narrow AI excels in one area, such as speech recognition, image classification, or game playing.

- **Predefined Functions**: It follows specific instructions and rules programmed by humans.

- **No Understanding**: Narrow AI does not possess an understanding or awareness beyond its specific task.

Examples of Narrow AI

- **Voice Assistants**: Siri, Alexa, and Google Assistant use narrow AI for voice recognition and responding to queries.

- **Recommendation Systems**: Netflix and Amazon use AI to suggest movies and products based on user preferences.

- **Self-Driving Cars**: Narrow AI is used to analyze the

environment and make driving decisions.

General AI

General AI, also known as strong AI or artificial general intelligence (AGI), refers to systems that possess the ability to understand, learn, and apply knowledge across a wide range of tasks, similar to human intelligence.

Characteristics of General AI

- **Human-Like Intelligence**: General AI can perform any intellectual task that a human can do.
- **Adaptability**: It can adapt to new situations and solve problems without human intervention.
- **Learning and Understanding**: General AI has the ability to learn from experiences and apply that knowledge to different tasks.

Current State of General AI

- **Research and Development**: General AI remains a theoretical concept, with ongoing research aimed at achieving this level of intelligence.
- **Challenges**: Developing AGI requires overcoming significant challenges, including understanding human cognition, building adaptable systems, and ensuring safety and ethics.

Superintelligent AI

Superintelligent AI, or artificial superintelligence (ASI), refers to systems that surpass human intelligence in all aspects, including creativity, problem-solving, and emotional intelligence.

Characteristics of Superintelligent AI

- **Superior Intelligence**: ASI exceeds human intelligence in every domain.

- **Self-Improvement**: It has the capability to improve itself autonomously, leading to rapid advancements.

- **Unpredictability**: The behavior and decisions of ASI could be unpredictable due to its superior cognitive abilities.

Potential Impacts of Superintelligent AI

- **Positive Impacts**: ASI could solve complex global challenges, such as curing diseases, addressing climate change, and advancing technology.

- **Risks and Concerns**: The development of ASI raises ethical and existential risks, including loss of human control and unintended consequences.

AI vs. Human Intelligence

Understanding the differences between AI and human intelligence is crucial for grasping the capabilities and limitations of AI systems.

Cognitive Abilities

- **Human Intelligence**: Humans possess a wide range of cognitive abilities, including reasoning, problem-solving, creativity, and emotional intelligence.

- **AI**: AI systems excel in specific tasks and data processing but lack the broad cognitive abilities and emotional understanding of humans.

Learning and Adaptation

- **Human Intelligence**: Humans learn from experiences, adapt to new situations, and apply knowledge across different contexts.
- **AI**: AI learns from data and algorithms, with limited ability to generalize knowledge across diverse tasks.

Creativity and Innovation

- **Human Intelligence**: Humans are capable of original thought, creativity, and innovation, producing new ideas and solutions.
- **AI**: AI can generate creative outputs based on patterns and data but lacks true originality and innovation.

Emotional Intelligence

- **Human Intelligence**: Humans possess emotional intelligence, including empathy, social skills, and self-awareness.
- **AI**: AI can recognize and respond to emotions to a limited extent but does not experience or understand emotions as humans do.

Decision-Making

- **Human Intelligence**: Humans make decisions based on a

combination of logic, intuition, and emotions.

- **AI**: AI makes decisions based on data and algorithms, often providing objective and data-driven insights.

Advantages and Limitations

- **Human Intelligence**: Humans have the advantage of flexibility, creativity, and emotional understanding but are limited by cognitive biases and information processing capacity.

- **AI**: AI excels in data processing, speed, and accuracy but is limited by its task-specific design, lack of generalization, and inability to understand context beyond its programming.

Integrating AI with Human Intelligence

The future of AI involves integrating AI with human intelligence to create systems that complement and enhance human capabilities.

Collaborative Intelligence

Collaborative intelligence involves humans and AI working together to achieve better outcomes than either could alone. This collaboration can take various forms, including:

- **Augmented Intelligence**: AI assists humans in decision-making, providing data-driven insights and recommendations.

- **Human-AI Teams**: Teams of humans and AI systems collaborate on complex tasks, leveraging the strengths of both.

- **Cognitive Assistants**: AI-powered assistants support humans in various activities, from medical diagnosis to customer service.

Enhancing Human Capabilities

AI can enhance human capabilities in several ways:

- **Enhanced Decision-Making**: AI provides valuable data insights, helping humans make informed decisions.
- **Increased Productivity**: AI automates repetitive tasks, allowing humans to focus on more creative and strategic activities.
- **Personalized Experiences**: AI enables personalized experiences in education, healthcare, and entertainment, tailored to individual needs and preferences.

Ethical and Responsible Integration

Integrating AI with human intelligence raises important ethical considerations:

- **Fairness and Bias**: Ensuring AI systems are fair and unbiased, avoiding discrimination and ensuring equal treatment.
- **Transparency**: Making AI systems transparent and understandable, allowing users to trust and interpret AI decisions.
- **Privacy and Security**: Protecting personal data and ensuring AI systems are secure from misuse and attacks.
- **Accountability**: Defining clear accountability for AI actions and decisions, ensuring human oversight and responsibility.

Summary

The foundations of AI encompass a wide range of concepts, from basic terminology to the different types of AI and their capabilities compared to human intelligence. Understanding these foundations is crucial for anyone interested in AI, as it provides the groundwork for exploring more advanced topics and applications. By integrating AI with human intelligence responsibly, we can unlock the potential of AI to enhance our lives and address complex global challenges.

CHAPTER 3: KEY TECHNOLOGIES IN AI

Machine Learning

Machine learning (ML) is a subset of artificial intelligence that focuses on the development of algorithms and statistical models that enable computers to learn from and make predictions or decisions based on data. ML is the driving force behind many modern AI applications and is divided into several types, including supervised learning, unsupervised learning, and reinforcement learning.

Supervised Learning

Supervised learning is a type of machine learning where the model is trained on a labeled dataset, meaning that each training example is paired with an output label. The goal is to learn a mapping from inputs to outputs that can generalize well to new, unseen data.

Key Concepts

- **Training Set**: A dataset used to train the model, containing input-output pairs.

- **Validation Set**: A dataset used to tune the model's hyperparameters and evaluate its performance during training.

- **Test Set**: A dataset used to assess the model's performance on new, unseen data.

- **Loss Function**: A function that measures the difference between the predicted output and the actual output. The goal is to minimize this function.

- **Optimization Algorithm**: An algorithm used to adjust the model's parameters to minimize the loss function. Common algorithms include gradient descent and its variants.

Common Algorithms

- **Linear Regression**: A simple algorithm used for predicting a continuous output based on a linear relationship between the input features and the output.

- **Logistic Regression**: An algorithm used for binary classification problems, where the output is a probability that the input belongs to a particular class.

- **Decision Trees**: A model that splits the data into subsets based on the value of input features, creating a tree-like structure of decisions.

- **Support Vector Machines (SVM)**: An algorithm that finds the hyperplane that best separates the data into different classes.

- **Neural Networks**: A set of algorithms modeled after the human brain, consisting of layers of interconnected nodes (neurons) that can learn complex patterns in the data.

Unsupervised Learning

Unsupervised learning is a type of machine learning where the model is trained on an unlabeled dataset, meaning that the data does not have predefined output labels. The goal is to find hidden patterns or structures in the data.

Key Concepts

- **Clustering**: The task of grouping similar data points together. The most common clustering algorithm is k-means.

- **Dimensionality Reduction**: Techniques used to reduce the number of input features while retaining the most important information. Common methods include Principal Component Analysis (PCA) and t-Distributed Stochastic Neighbor Embedding (t-SNE).

- **Association**: Identifying relationships between variables in large datasets. The Apriori algorithm is commonly used for this purpose.

Common Algorithms

- **K-Means Clustering**: An algorithm that partitions the data into k clusters, where each data point belongs to the cluster with the nearest mean.

- **Hierarchical Clustering**: A method of clustering that builds a hierarchy of clusters by either merging small clusters into larger ones (agglomerative) or splitting large clusters into smaller ones (divisive).

- **Principal Component Analysis (PCA)**: A technique used to reduce the dimensionality of the data by projecting it onto a lower-dimensional subspace.

- **Autoencoders**: A type of neural network used for dimensionality reduction and feature learning by encoding the input data into a lower-dimensional representation and then decoding it back to the original dimension.

Reinforcement Learning

Reinforcement learning (RL) is a type of machine learning where an agent learns to make decisions by interacting with its environment and receiving rewards or penalties for its actions. The goal is to learn a policy that maximizes the cumulative reward over time.

Key Concepts

- **Agent**: The entity that makes decisions and takes actions in the environment.

- **Environment**: The system with which the agent interacts and receives feedback.

- **State**: A representation of the current situation or context of the agent within the environment.

- **Action**: A move or decision made by the agent that affects the state of the environment.

- **Reward**: Feedback received by the agent after taking an action, used to evaluate its performance.

- **Policy**: A strategy used by the agent to decide which actions to take in different states.

- **Value Function**: A function that estimates the expected cumulative reward for a given state or state-action pair.

- **Q-Learning**: A model-free reinforcement learning algorithm that learns the value of taking a particular action in a particular state.

Common Algorithms

- **Q-Learning**: An off-policy algorithm that learns the value of actions in different states by updating Q-values based on the reward received.

- **SARSA (State-Action-Reward-State-Action)**: An on-policy algorithm that updates Q-values based on the action actually taken by the agent.

- **Deep Q-Networks (DQN)**: A variant of Q-learning that uses deep neural networks to approximate the Q-values.

- **Policy Gradient Methods**: Algorithms that directly optimize the policy by adjusting the parameters to maximize the expected cumulative reward.

- **Actor-Critic Methods**: A combination of policy gradient and value function methods, where the actor updates the policy and the critic evaluates the action taken by the actor.

Neural Networks and Deep Learning

Neural networks and deep learning are key technologies in AI that enable the development of sophisticated models capable of learning complex patterns in data.

Neural Networks

Neural networks are a set of algorithms modeled after the human brain, consisting of layers of interconnected nodes (neurons) that can learn complex patterns in the data.

Key Concepts

- **Neuron**: The basic unit of a neural network, which receives input, processes it, and produces output.

- **Layer**: A group of neurons that operate at the same level in the network. Common types of layers include input layers, hidden layers, and output layers.

- **Activation Function**: A function applied to the output of a neuron to introduce non-linearity into the network. Common activation functions include ReLU, sigmoid, and tanh.

- **Feedforward Neural Network**: A type of neural network where connections between neurons do not form cycles, with information flowing in one direction from input to output.

- **Backpropagation**: An algorithm used to train neural networks by calculating the gradient of the loss function with respect to each weight and updating the weights to minimize the loss.

Common Architectures

- **Fully Connected Networks (FCN)**: A type of neural network where each neuron in one layer is connected to every neuron in the next layer.

- **Convolutional Neural Networks (CNN)**: A type of neural network designed for processing structured grid data like images, using convolutional layers to capture spatial patterns.

- **Recurrent Neural Networks (RNN)**: A type of neural network designed for sequential data, where connections between neurons form directed cycles to capture temporal dependencies.

- **Long Short-Term Memory (LSTM)**: A variant of RNN designed to address the vanishing gradient problem, capable of learning long-term dependencies.

Deep Learning

Deep learning is a subset of machine learning that involves neural networks with many layers (deep neural networks). It is used for more complex tasks like image and speech recognition.

Key Concepts

- **Deep Neural Network (DNN)**: A neural network with multiple hidden layers between the input and output layers.

- **Training**: The process of feeding data into the neural network and adjusting the weights to minimize the loss function.

- **Epoch**: One complete pass through the entire training dataset.

- **Batch Size**: The number of training examples used in one iteration of training.

- **Overfitting**: A situation where the model learns the training data too well, including noise and outliers, resulting in poor generalization to new data.

- **Regularization**: Techniques used to prevent overfitting by adding constraints to the model, such as L1 and L2 regularization, dropout, and data augmentation.

Common Applications

- **Image Recognition**: Deep learning models can classify images, detect objects, and recognize faces with high accuracy.

- **Speech Recognition**: Deep learning models can transcribe spoken language into text, enabling applications like virtual assistants and transcription services.

- **Natural Language Processing (NLP)**: Deep learning models can understand and generate human language, enabling applications like chatbots, language translation, and sentiment analysis.

- **Recommendation Systems**: Deep learning models can analyze user preferences and recommend products, movies, and music.

Natural Language Processing

Natural Language Processing (NLP) is a field of AI that focuses on the interaction between computers and human language. It involves the development of algorithms and models that enable machines to understand, interpret, and generate human language.

Key Concepts

- **Tokenization**: The process of breaking down text into smaller units, such as words or sentences.

- **Part-of-Speech (POS) Tagging**: The process of labeling each word in a sentence with its corresponding part of speech, such as noun, verb, or adjective.

- **Named Entity Recognition (NER)**: The process of identifying and classifying entities, such as names of people, organizations, and locations, in a text.

- **Sentiment Analysis**: The process of determining the sentiment or emotion expressed in a text, such as positive, negative, or neutral.

- **Machine Translation**: The process of translating text from one language to another using AI models.

- **Text Generation**: The process of generating coherent and contextually relevant text based on a given input.

Common Algorithms and Models

- **Bag-of-Words (BoW)**: A simple model that represents text as a collection of words without considering their order.

- **TF-IDF (Term Frequency-Inverse Document Frequency)**: A

model that represents text based on the importance of words, calculated using their frequency in the document and across the entire dataset.

- **Word Embeddings**: Dense vector representations of words that capture their semantic meanings and relationships. Common models include Word2Vec, GloVe, and FastText.

- **Recurrent Neural Networks (RNN)**: A type of neural network designed for sequential data, commonly used for tasks like language modeling and machine translation.

- **Transformers**: A neural network architecture that uses self-attention mechanisms to capture long-range dependencies in text. It is the basis for state-of-the-art models like BERT, GPT, and T5.

Applications

- **Chatbots and Virtual Assistants**: NLP enables chatbots and virtual assistants to understand and respond to user queries in natural language.

- **Sentiment Analysis**: NLP is used to analyze customer reviews, social media posts, and other textual data to determine sentiment and opinion.

- **Language Translation**: NLP models are used to translate text between different languages, enabling communication across language barriers.

- **Text Summarization**: NLP is used to generate concise summaries of long documents, making it easier to extract key information.

- **Information Retrieval**: NLP is used to improve search engines and recommendation systems by understanding the context and intent behind user queries.

Computer Vision

Computer vision is a field of AI that focuses on enabling machines to interpret and understand visual information from the world, such as images and videos.

Key Concepts

- **Image Classification**: The task of assigning a label to an entire image based on its content.

- **Object Detection**: The task of identifying and localizing objects within an image.

- **Semantic Segmentation**: The task of assigning a label to each pixel in an image, resulting in a detailed classification of different regions.

- **Instance Segmentation**: A combination of object detection and semantic segmentation, where each object instance is segmented and labeled separately.

- **Feature Extraction**: The process of identifying and extracting important features from an image, such as edges, corners, and textures.

Common Algorithms and Models

- **Convolutional Neural Networks (CNN)**: A type of neural network specifically designed for processing structured grid data like images. CNNs use convolutional layers to capture spatial patterns.

- **ResNet (Residual Networks)**: A deep learning model that introduces skip connections to enable the training of very deep networks.

- **YOLO (You Only Look Once)**: A real-time object detection model that predicts bounding boxes and class probabilities for objects in an image.

- **Mask R-CNN**: A model that combines object detection and semantic segmentation to perform instance segmentation.

- **Generative Adversarial Networks (GANs)**: A type of neural network used for generating realistic images by training two networks, a generator and a discriminator, in a competitive manner.

Applications

- **Image Recognition**: Computer vision models can classify images into predefined categories, enabling applications like facial recognition and medical image analysis.

- **Object Detection**: Computer vision models can detect and localize objects in images, enabling applications like autonomous driving and surveillance.

- **Image Segmentation**: Computer vision models can segment images into different regions, enabling applications like medical imaging and scene understanding.

- **Image Generation**: Computer vision models can generate realistic images, enabling applications like art creation and data augmentation.

- **Augmented Reality (AR) and Virtual Reality (VR)**: Computer vision is used to create immersive AR and VR experiences by understanding and interacting with the visual environment.

Robotics

Robotics is a field of AI that focuses on the design, construction, and operation of robots that can perform tasks autonomously or semi-autonomously.

Key Concepts

- **Robot**: A machine capable of carrying out a complex series of actions automatically, especially one programmable by a computer.
- **Actuators**: Components that convert electrical signals into physical movement, enabling the robot to interact with its environment.
- **Sensors**: Devices that collect information from the environment, such as cameras, microphones, and pressure sensors.
- **Control Systems**: Algorithms and mechanisms that control the movement and actions of the robot based on sensor input.
- **Path Planning**: The process of determining a path for the robot to follow to reach a specific goal.
- **Localization and Mapping**: The process of determining the robot's position in its environment and creating a map of the surroundings.

Common Algorithms and Models

- **Kinematics**: The study of motion without considering the forces that cause it, used to model and control the movement of robots.
- **Inverse Kinematics**: The process of determining the joint angles required for the robot to achieve a desired position and orientation.
- **Probabilistic Robotics**: A framework that uses probability theory to model and manage the uncertainty in robot perception and action.

- **Simultaneous Localization and Mapping (SLAM)**: An algorithm that enables a robot to build a map of an unknown environment while simultaneously keeping track of its location.

- **Reinforcement Learning**: A type of machine learning where a robot learns to perform tasks by interacting with its environment and receiving rewards or penalties for its actions.

Applications

- **Manufacturing**: Robots are used for tasks like assembly, welding, and painting in manufacturing processes, improving efficiency and precision.

- **Healthcare**: Robots assist in surgeries, rehabilitation, and patient care, enhancing the quality of healthcare services.

- **Autonomous Vehicles**: Self-driving cars use robotics and AI to navigate and interact with the environment, aiming to improve transportation safety and efficiency.

- **Service Robots**: Robots perform tasks like cleaning, delivery, and customer service, providing convenience and support in various settings.

- **Exploration**: Robots are used for exploring hazardous environments, such as deep-sea exploration and space missions, where human presence is challenging.

Summary

In this chapter, we have explored the key technologies in AI, including machine learning, neural networks, deep learning, natural language processing, computer vision, and robotics. Each technology plays a crucial role in the development and application of AI systems, enabling machines to learn, understand, and interact with the world in increasingly sophisticated ways. As we continue to delve deeper into the world of AI, understanding these foundational technologies will provide the necessary knowledge to appreciate the full potential and implications of artificial intelligence.

CHAPTER 4: AI TOOLS AND PLATFORMS

Introduction to AI Tools and Platforms

The development and deployment of AI systems require a diverse set of tools and platforms. These tools facilitate various stages of the AI lifecycle, from data preparation and model building to deployment and monitoring. In this chapter, we will explore the most popular AI frameworks, libraries, cloud-based services, and the necessary environment setup for AI projects.

Why AI Tools and Platforms Are Essential

AI tools and platforms are crucial for several reasons:

1. **Efficiency**: They streamline the development process, allowing researchers and developers to build, train, and deploy models faster.

2. **Scalability**: Cloud-based platforms enable the handling of large datasets and complex computations, making it easier to scale AI applications.

3. **Collaboration**: Many platforms offer collaborative features that facilitate teamwork among data scientists, engineers, and stakeholders.

4. **Ease of Use**: Modern AI tools often come with user-friendly

interfaces and pre-built models that lower the barrier to entry for beginners.

5. **Integration**: These tools integrate well with other software and systems, making it easier to incorporate AI into existing workflows.

Popular AI Frameworks and Libraries

Several frameworks and libraries are widely used in AI development due to their robustness, flexibility, and community support. Here, we discuss some of the most prominent ones.

TensorFlow

TensorFlow is an open-source machine learning framework developed by the Google Brain team. It is widely used for a range of tasks, including deep learning, machine learning, and statistical modeling.

Key Features

- **Flexibility**: TensorFlow supports multiple languages, including Python, C++, and JavaScript.

- **Scalability**: It can run on various platforms, from mobile devices to large-scale distributed systems.

- **Ecosystem**: TensorFlow has a rich ecosystem, including TensorFlow Lite for mobile and embedded devices, TensorFlow.js for JavaScript applications, and TensorFlow Extended (TFX) for end-to-end ML pipelines.

Getting Started

To get started with TensorFlow, you need to install it using pip:

```sh
pip install tensorflow
```

Here's a simple example of building and training a neural network in TensorFlow:

```
import tensorflow as tf
from tensorflow.keras import layers, models

# Load and preprocess the dataset
(train_images, train_labels), (test_images, test_labels) = tf.keras.datasets.mnist.load_data()
train_images = train_images / 255.0
test_images = test_images / 255.0

# Build the model
model = models.Sequential([
    layers.Flatten(input_shape=(28, 28)),
    layers.Dense(128, activation='relu'),
    layers.Dense(10, activation='softmax')
])

# Compile the model
model.compile(optimizer='adam',
              loss='sparse_categorical_crossentropy',
```

```
              metrics=['accuracy'])

# Train the model
model.fit(train_images, train_labels, epochs=5)

# Evaluate the model
test_loss, test_acc = model.evaluate(test_images, test_labels)
print(f'Test accuracy: {test_acc}')

```python
import tensorflow as tf
from tensorflow.keras import layers, models

# Load and preprocess the dataset
(train_images, train_labels), (test_images, test_labels) = tf.keras.datasets.mnist.load_data()
train_images = train_images / 255.0
test_images = test_images / 255.0

# Build the model
model = models.Sequential([
    layers.Flatten(input_shape=(28, 28)),
    layers.Dense(128, activation='relu'),
    layers.Dense(10, activation='softmax')
])

# Compile the model
model.compile(optimizer='adam',
              loss='sparse_categorical_crossentropy',
```
```

                metrics=['accuracy'])

# Train the model
model.fit(train_images, train_labels, epochs=5)

Evaluate the model
test_loss, test_acc = model.evaluate(test_images, test_labels)
print(f'Test accuracy: {test_acc}')
```

## PyTorch

**PyTorch** is an open-source deep learning framework developed by Facebook's AI Research lab. It is known for its dynamic computation graph, which makes it flexible and easier to debug.

### Key Features

- **Dynamic Computation Graph**: Unlike static graphs used in TensorFlow, PyTorch's dynamic graphs allow for more flexibility and ease of use.
- **Ease of Use**: PyTorch's syntax is more intuitive for Python developers, making it a popular choice for research and development.
- **Integration**: PyTorch integrates well with other Python libraries and tools, such as NumPy and SciPy.

### Getting Started

To get started with PyTorch, you need to install it using pip:
```

```sh
pip install torch torchvision
```

Here's a simple example of building and training a neural network in PyTorch:

```python
import torch
import torch.nn as nn
import torch.optim as optim
from torchvision import datasets, transforms

# Define the neural network model
class Net(nn.Module):
    def __init__(self):
        super(Net, self).__init__()
        self.fc1 = nn.Linear(28*28, 128)
        self.fc2 = nn.Linear(128, 10)

    def forward(self, x):
        x = torch.flatten(x, 1)
        x = torch.relu(self.fc1(x))
        x = self.fc2(x)
        return x

# Load and preprocess the dataset
transform = transforms.Compose([transforms.ToTensor(),
```

```
                   transforms.Normalize((0.5,), (0.5,))])
trainset = datasets.MNIST('.', download=True, train=True,
transform=transform)
trainloader       =       torch.utils.data.DataLoader(trainset,
batch_size=64, shuffle=True)
testset = datasets.MNIST('.', download=True, train=False,
transform=transform)
testloader = torch.utils.data.DataLoader(testset, batch_size=64,
shuffle=False)

# Instantiate the model, loss function, and optimizer
model = Net()
criterion = nn.CrossEntropyLoss()
optimizer = optim.Adam(model.parameters())

# Train the model
for epoch in range(5):
    for images, labels in trainloader:
        optimizer.zero_grad()
        output = model(images)
        loss = criterion(output, labels)
        loss.backward()
        optimizer.step()

# Evaluate the model
correct = 0
total = 0
with torch.no_grad():
    for images, labels in testloader:
```

```
        output = model(images)
        _, predicted = torch.max(output, 1)
        total += labels.size(0)
        correct += (predicted == labels).sum().item()

print(f'Test accuracy: {correct / total}')
```

Keras

Keras is a high-level neural networks API, written in Python and capable of running on top of TensorFlow, Microsoft Cognitive Toolkit (CNTK), or Theano. It is designed to enable fast experimentation with deep learning models.

Key Features

- **User-Friendly**: Keras provides a simple and intuitive API for building and training models.
- **Modularity**: It is modular, making it easy to create complex models by combining different components.
- **Compatibility**: Keras is compatible with multiple backends, allowing flexibility in choosing the underlying framework.

Getting Started

To get started with Keras, you need to install it along with a backend like TensorFlow:

```sh
pip install keras tensorflow
```

```

Here's a simple example of building and training a neural network in Keras:

```python
from keras.datasets import mnist
from keras.models import Sequential
from keras.layers import Dense, Flatten
from keras.utils import to_categorical

# Load and preprocess the dataset
(train_images, train_labels), (test_images, test_labels) = mnist.load_data()
train_images = train_images / 255.0
test_images = test_images / 255.0
train_labels = to_categorical(train_labels)
test_labels = to_categorical(test_labels)

# Build the model
model = Sequential([
    Flatten(input_shape=(28, 28)),
    Dense(128, activation='relu'),
    Dense(10, activation='softmax')
])

# Compile the model
model.compile(optimizer='adam',
              loss='categorical_crossentropy',
```
```

              metrics=['accuracy'])

# Train the model
model.fit(train_images, train_labels, epochs=5)

Evaluate the model
test_loss, test_acc = model.evaluate(test_images, test_labels)
print(f'Test accuracy: {test_acc}')
```

## Scikit-Learn

**Scikit-Learn** is an open-source machine learning library for Python. It provides simple and efficient tools for data mining and data analysis.

### Key Features

- **Wide Range of Algorithms**: Scikit-Learn offers a variety of supervised and unsupervised learning algorithms.
- **Ease of Use**: It provides a consistent interface and easy-to-understand documentation.
- **Integration**": Scikit-Learn integrates well with other scientific libraries like NumPy and pandas.

### Getting Started

To get started with Scikit-Learn, you need to install it using pip:

```sh
pip install scikit-learn

Here's a simple example of building and training a machine learning model in Scikit-Learn:

```python
from sklearn.datasets import load_iris
from sklearn.model_selection import train_test_split
from sklearn.ensemble import RandomForestClassifier
from sklearn.metrics import accuracy_score

# Load and preprocess the dataset
data = load_iris()
X_train, X_test, y_train, y_test = train_test_split(data.data, data.target, test_size=0.2, random_state=42)

# Instantiate and train the model
model = RandomForestClassifier()
model.fit(X_train, y_train)

# Evaluate the model
predictions = model.predict(X_test)
print(f'Test accuracy: {accuracy_score(y_test, predictions)}')
```

Cloud-Based AI Services

Cloud-based AI services provide scalable, cost-effective solutions for deploying and managing AI models. These services are offered by major cloud providers, including Google Cloud,

Amazon Web Services (AWS), and Microsoft Azure.

Google Cloud AI

Google Cloud offers a suite of AI and machine learning services, including:

- **AutoML**: A suite of products that allows developers to train high-quality custom machine learning models with minimal effort and machine learning expertise.
- **AI Platform**: A comprehensive suite for building, training, and deploying ML models.
- **Vision AI**: A service for image recognition and analysis.
- **Natural Language AI**: A service for text analysis, including sentiment analysis, entity recognition, and language translation.

Getting Started

To get started with Google Cloud AI, you need to create a Google Cloud account and enable the relevant APIs. Here's an example of using the Vision AI service:

```python
from google.cloud import vision
import io

# Initialize the Vision client
client = vision.ImageAnnotatorClient()

# Load the image
```

```
with io.open('path/to/image.jpg', 'rb') as image_file:
    content = image_file.read()

image = vision.Image(content=content)

# Perform label detection
response = client.label_detection(image=image)
labels = response.label_annotations

# Print the labels
for label in labels:
    print(label.description)
```

Amazon Web Services (AWS) AI

AWS offers a range of AI services, including:

- **SageMaker**: A fully managed service for building, training, and deploying ML models.
- **Rekognition**: A service for image and video analysis.
- **Comprehend**: A service for natural language processing and text analysis.
- **Polly**: A service that converts text to lifelike speech.

Getting Started

To get started with AWS AI, you need to create an AWS account and set up the necessary credentials. Here's an example of using the Rekognition service:

```python
import boto3

# Initialize the Rekognition client
client = boto3.client('rekognition')

# Load the image
with open('path/to/image.jpg', 'rb') as image_file:
    image_bytes = image_file.read()

# Perform label detection
response = client.detect_labels(Image={'Bytes': image_bytes})

# Print the labels
for label in response['Labels']:
    print(label['Name'])
```

Microsoft Azure AI

Azure offers a variety of AI and machine learning services, including:

- **Azure Machine Learning**: A cloud-based environment for training, deploying, and managing ML models.
- **Cognitive Services**: A collection of APIs for vision, speech, language, and decision-making tasks.
- **Bot Service**: A platform for building and deploying chatbots.

Getting Started

To get started with Azure AI, you need to create an Azure account and set up the necessary resources. Here's an example of using the Cognitive Services Computer Vision API:

```python
import requests

# Set up the API endpoint and subscription key
endpoint = 'https://<your-resource-name>.cognitiveservices.azure.com/'
subscription_key = '<your-subscription-key>'

# Load the image
image_path = 'path/to/image.jpg'
with open(image_path, 'rb') as image_file:
    image_data = image_file.read()

# Perform label detection
headers = {'Ocp-Apim-Subscription-Key': subscription_key, 'Content-Type': 'application/octet-stream'}
params = {'visualFeatures': 'Categories,Description,Color'}
response = requests.post(endpoint + 'vision/v3.0/analyze', headers=headers, params=params, data=image_data)
analysis = response.json()

# Print the labels
for category in analysis['categories']:
```

        print(category['name'])
```

Setting Up Your AI Environment

To effectively work on AI projects, you need to set up a development environment that includes the necessary tools, libraries, and resources. This section covers the essential steps to set up an AI environment.

Hardware Requirements

AI development often requires significant computational resources, especially for training deep learning models. Key hardware components include:

- **CPU**: Central Processing Unit for general computing tasks.

- **GPU**: Graphics Processing Unit for accelerating deep learning tasks.

- **RAM**: Sufficient memory to handle large datasets and complex models.

- **Storage**: Adequate storage for datasets and model checkpoints.

Software Requirements

The software stack for AI development includes operating systems, programming languages, and libraries.

Operating Systems

- **Linux**: Preferred by many AI researchers and developers for
```

its stability and support for development tools.

- **Windows**: Supported by major AI frameworks and tools.
- **macOS**: Suitable for development, though some tools may have limited support.

Programming Languages

- **Python**: The most popular language for AI development due to its simplicity and extensive library support.
- **R**: Preferred for statistical analysis and data visualization.
- **C++**: Used for performance-critical components in AI systems.

Development Tools

Integrated Development Environments (IDEs)

- **PyCharm**: A popular IDE for Python development with support for AI libraries.
- **Jupyter Notebook**: An interactive environment for running and sharing code, widely used in AI research.
- **Visual Studio Code**: A lightweight code editor with support for Python and other languages.

Version Control Systems

- **Git**: A widely used version control system for tracking changes and collaborating on code.

Docker

Docker is a containerization platform that allows you to package applications and their dependencies into isolated containers, ensuring consistency across development and production environments.

Installing and Setting Up Libraries

To get started with AI development, you need to install the necessary libraries. Here's a guide to setting up a basic AI environment with TensorFlow, PyTorch, and other essential libraries.

Step-by-Step Guide

1. **Install Python**: Download and install the latest version of Python from the official website.

2. **Create a Virtual Environment**: Use `venv` or `conda` to create an isolated environment for your project.

```sh
python -m venv myenv
source myenv/bin/activate   # On Windows: myenv\Scripts\activate
```

3. **Install TensorFlow**:

```sh
pip install tensorflow
```

4. **Install PyTorch**:

   ```sh
   pip install torch torchvision
   ```

5. **Install Keras**:

   ```sh
   pip install keras
   ```

6. **Install Scikit-Learn**:

   ```sh
   pip install scikit-learn
   ```

7. **Install Jupyter Notebook**:

   ```sh
   pip install jupyter
   jupyter notebook
   ```

Setting Up Cloud Environments

For larger projects and production deployments, using cloud environments can provide scalability and computational power.

Here's how to set up an AI environment on Google Cloud, AWS, and Azure.

Google Cloud

1. **Create a Google Cloud Account**: Sign up for Google Cloud and create a new project.

2. **Set Up a VM Instance**: Create a virtual machine instance with the desired specifications (CPU, GPU, RAM).

3. **Install AI Libraries**: SSH into the VM and install the necessary AI libraries (TensorFlow, PyTorch, etc.).

```sh
sudo apt-get update
sudo apt-get install python3-pip
pip3 install tensorflow torch torchvision
```

4. **Use AI Services**: Enable and configure Google Cloud AI services like AutoML and AI Platform.

Amazon Web Services (AWS)

1. **Create an AWS Account**: Sign up for AWS and create a new user with administrative privileges.

2. **Set Up an EC2 Instance**: Launch an EC2 instance with the desired specifications.

3. **Install AI Libraries**: SSH into the instance and install the

necessary AI libraries.

```sh
sudo yum update
sudo yum install python3-pip
pip3 install tensorflow torch torchvision
```

4. **Use AI Services**: Set up and configure AWS AI services like SageMaker, Rekognition, and Comprehend.

Microsoft Azure

1. **Create an Azure Account**: Sign up for Azure and create a new resource group.

2. **Set Up a VM Instance**: Create a virtual machine with the desired specifications.

3. **Install AI Libraries**: SSH into the VM and install the necessary AI libraries.

```sh
sudo apt-get update
sudo apt-get install python3-pip
pip3 install tensorflow torch torchvision
```

4. **Use AI Services**: Enable and configure Azure AI services like Azure Machine Learning and Cognitive Services.

Summary

In this chapter, we have explored the essential tools and platforms for AI development. These include popular frameworks and libraries like TensorFlow, PyTorch, Keras, and Scikit-Learn, as well as cloud-based AI services from Google Cloud, AWS, and Microsoft Azure. Setting up a proper AI environment, both locally and on the cloud, is crucial for the efficient development and deployment of AI models. As you continue your journey in AI, leveraging these tools and platforms will enable you to build robust, scalable, and efficient AI systems.

CHAPTER 5: APPLICATIONS OF AI

Artificial Intelligence (AI) is transforming various sectors by automating processes, enhancing decision-making, and creating new opportunities for innovation. In this chapter, we will explore the diverse applications of AI across different industries, including healthcare, finance, transportation, entertainment, and education. Each section will delve into specific use cases, illustrating how AI is driving advancements and addressing challenges in these fields.

AI in Healthcare

AI is revolutionizing healthcare by improving diagnostics, personalizing treatment, and enhancing operational efficiency. Here, we examine some of the most impactful applications of AI in the healthcare industry.

Diagnostics and Imaging

AI-powered diagnostic tools and imaging systems are enhancing the accuracy and speed of disease detection.

Medical Imaging

- **Radiology**: AI algorithms analyze medical images such as

X-rays, MRIs, and CT scans to identify abnormalities, such as tumors, fractures, and infections, with high accuracy. For example, AI systems can detect breast cancer in mammograms earlier than human radiologists.

- **Pathology**: AI is used to examine tissue samples and identify pathological features in diseases like cancer. Digital pathology, combined with AI, enables faster and more accurate diagnosis.

Predictive Analytics

- **Early Detection**: AI models analyze patient data, including medical history and genetic information, to predict the likelihood of diseases like diabetes, heart disease, and cancer. Early detection allows for timely intervention and better patient outcomes.

- **Risk Stratification**: AI helps in identifying high-risk patients by analyzing electronic health records (EHRs) and other data sources. This enables healthcare providers to prioritize care and allocate resources efficiently.

Personalized Medicine

AI is enabling personalized treatment plans tailored to individual patients' genetic makeup and health profiles.

Pharmacogenomics

- **Drug Response Prediction**: AI analyzes genetic data to predict how patients will respond to different medications. This helps in selecting the most effective drug with minimal side effects.

- **Drug Development**: AI accelerates the drug discovery process by identifying potential drug candidates and predicting their efficacy and safety.

Treatment Optimization

- **Personalized Treatment Plans**: AI algorithms recommend personalized treatment plans based on patient data, including demographics, medical history, and lifestyle factors. This improves treatment efficacy and reduces adverse effects.

- **Chronic Disease Management**: AI-powered applications monitor patients with chronic conditions, such as diabetes and hypertension, and provide personalized recommendations for managing their health.

Operational Efficiency

AI is streamlining administrative and operational processes in healthcare, leading to cost savings and improved patient care.

Workflow Automation

- **Administrative Tasks**: AI automates routine administrative tasks, such as appointment scheduling, billing, and insurance claims processing. This reduces the workload on healthcare staff and minimizes errors.

- **Clinical Documentation**: Natural Language Processing (NLP) tools assist in documenting patient interactions and updating EHRs, allowing healthcare providers to focus more on patient care.

Resource Management

- **Hospital Operations**: AI optimizes hospital operations by predicting patient admissions, managing bed occupancy, and scheduling staff shifts. This ensures efficient use of resources and improves patient care.

- **Supply Chain Management**: AI algorithms forecast demand for medical supplies and optimize inventory management, reducing waste and ensuring timely availability of essential items.

AI in Finance

The finance industry is leveraging AI to enhance fraud detection, risk management, customer service, and investment strategies. This section explores the key applications of AI in finance.

Fraud Detection and Prevention

AI systems are highly effective in detecting and preventing fraudulent activities in financial transactions.

Anomaly Detection

- **Transaction Monitoring**: AI algorithms monitor financial transactions in real-time to identify unusual patterns that may indicate fraud. Machine learning models can learn from historical data to distinguish between legitimate and fraudulent activities.

- **Account Security**: AI-powered security systems detect unauthorized access and suspicious account activities, helping to prevent identity theft and account takeovers.

Risk Assessment

- **Credit Scoring**: AI enhances traditional credit scoring models by incorporating a wider range of data sources, such as social media activity and transaction history, to assess the creditworthiness of individuals and businesses.

- **Loan Approval**: AI algorithms analyze borrower data to assess risk and make more informed loan approval decisions, reducing default rates and improving lending efficiency.

Investment and Trading

AI is transforming investment strategies and trading practices through data analysis and predictive modeling.

Algorithmic Trading

- **Automated Trading**: AI-driven trading algorithms execute trades at high speeds and with precision, capitalizing on market opportunities that may be missed by human traders. These algorithms analyze market data, news, and social media to make trading decisions.

- **Quantitative Analysis**: AI models analyze vast amounts of financial data to identify patterns and trends, providing insights for quantitative trading strategies.

Portfolio Management

- **Robo-Advisors**: AI-powered robo-advisors provide personalized investment advice and portfolio management services to individual investors. These platforms use algorithms to assess risk tolerance, financial goals, and market conditions to create optimized investment portfolios.

- **Risk Management**: AI helps portfolio managers assess and manage risk by analyzing market conditions, asset correlations, and macroeconomic factors. This enables more effective diversification and risk mitigation strategies.

Customer Service and Personalization

AI enhances customer service and personalization in the finance industry through chatbots, virtual assistants, and personalized financial advice.

Chatbots and Virtual Assistants

- **24/7 Support**: AI-powered chatbots provide round-the-clock customer support, handling routine inquiries, transaction requests, and account management tasks. This improves customer satisfaction and reduces the workload on human agents.

- **Natural Language Processing**: NLP enables chatbots and virtual assistants to understand and respond to customer queries in natural language, providing a more intuitive and user-friendly experience.

Personalized Financial Advice

- **Personal Finance Management**: AI-powered applications analyze user spending habits, income, and financial goals to provide personalized budgeting and saving recommendations. These tools help users make informed financial decisions and achieve their financial goals.

- **Wealth Management**: AI-driven platforms offer personalized wealth management services, including investment advice, retirement planning, and tax optimization. These services are tailored to individual financial profiles and objectives.

AI in Transportation

AI is playing a pivotal role in transforming the transportation industry by enhancing safety, efficiency, and sustainability. This section explores the key applications of AI in transportation.

Autonomous Vehicles

Autonomous vehicles (AVs) are one of the most significant advancements in AI, promising to revolutionize transportation.

Self-Driving Cars

- **Perception and Navigation**: AI systems enable self-driving cars to perceive their environment through sensors like cameras, LiDAR, and radar. These systems process sensor data to detect obstacles, traffic signals, and road markings, allowing the vehicle to navigate safely.

- **Decision-Making**: AI algorithms analyze real-time data to make driving decisions, such as lane changes, turns, and speed adjustments. These algorithms prioritize safety and compliance with traffic laws.

Public Transportation

- **Autonomous Buses**: AI is being used to develop autonomous buses that can navigate urban environments, pick up passengers, and adhere to schedules without human intervention. These buses aim to improve public transportation efficiency and reduce operational costs.

- **Last-Mile Delivery**: Autonomous delivery vehicles and drones are being developed to handle last-mile deliveries, reducing delivery times and costs while improving logistics efficiency.

Traffic Management

AI is improving traffic management systems to enhance road safety and reduce congestion.

Intelligent Traffic Control

- **Adaptive Traffic Signals**: AI-powered traffic signals adjust their timing based on real-time traffic conditions, optimizing traffic flow and reducing congestion. These systems use data from cameras, sensors, and GPS to make adjustments.
- **Incident Detection**: AI systems monitor traffic conditions and detect incidents such as accidents or breakdowns. These systems alert authorities and provide real-time information to drivers, helping to minimize delays and improve response times.

Traffic Prediction

- **Predictive Analytics**: AI models analyze historical traffic data and current conditions to predict traffic patterns and congestion. This information is used to optimize traffic management strategies and provide real-time traffic updates to drivers.
- **Route Optimization**: AI-powered navigation systems recommend optimal routes based on real-time traffic data, helping drivers avoid congestion and reduce travel times.

Fleet Management

AI is enhancing fleet management by optimizing routes,

reducing fuel consumption, and improving maintenance.

Route Optimization

- **Dynamic Routing**: AI algorithms optimize delivery and service routes based on real-time traffic conditions, weather, and delivery constraints. This reduces fuel consumption, travel time, and operational costs.

- **Predictive Maintenance**: AI systems monitor vehicle performance and predict maintenance needs, preventing breakdowns and extending the lifespan of fleet vehicles. This proactive approach reduces downtime and maintenance costs.

Fuel Efficiency

- **Eco-Driving**: AI-powered systems provide feedback to drivers on fuel-efficient driving practices, such as optimal acceleration and braking patterns. These systems help reduce fuel consumption and emissions.

- **Telematics**: AI analyzes telematics data from fleet vehicles to identify areas for improving fuel efficiency, such as route adjustments and vehicle maintenance.

AI in Entertainment

The entertainment industry is leveraging AI to create immersive experiences, personalize content, and streamline production processes. This section explores the key applications of AI in entertainment.

Content Creation and Personalization

AI is transforming content creation and personalization in

the entertainment industry, enhancing user experiences and engagement.

Content Recommendation

- **Personalized Recommendations**: AI algorithms analyze user preferences, viewing history, and behavior to provide personalized content recommendations. Streaming platforms like Netflix and Spotify use these algorithms to suggest movies, shows, and music tailored to individual tastes.
- **Collaborative Filtering**: This technique identifies patterns in user behavior and preferences to recommend content that similar users have enjoyed. It helps in discovering new and relevant content for users.

Content Generation

- **Automated Content Creation**: AI is being used to generate content, such as news articles, music, and art. Natural Language Generation (NLG) tools can create news summaries and reports, while AI-driven music composition tools can create original music tracks.
- **Deepfake Technology**: AI algorithms create realistic synthetic media, such as videos and images, by altering existing content or generating new content. This technology is being used for special effects in movies and virtual reality experiences.

Gaming and Virtual Reality

AI is enhancing gaming experiences and virtual reality (VR) applications by creating intelligent and immersive environments.

Game Design

- **Procedural Content Generation**: AI algorithms generate game content, such as levels, characters, and storylines, dynamically. This allows for more diverse and replayable gaming experiences.

- **Non-Player Characters (NPCs)**: AI enables NPCs to exhibit realistic behaviors and interactions, enhancing the overall gaming experience. These characters can adapt to player actions and provide dynamic challenges.

Virtual Reality

- **Immersive Experiences**: AI enhances VR experiences by creating realistic environments and interactions. Machine learning algorithms can simulate real-world physics, lighting, and textures, providing a more immersive experience.

- **Training and Simulation**: AI-powered VR applications are used for training and simulation in various fields, such as military, aviation, and healthcare. These applications provide realistic scenarios for practicing skills and decision-making.

Film and Media Production

AI is streamlining film and media production processes, improving efficiency and creativity.

Video Editing

- **Automated Editing**: AI tools assist in video editing by automating tasks such as scene detection, color correction, and audio enhancement. This speeds up the editing process and allows editors to focus on creative aspects.

- **Content Analysis**: AI analyzes video content to identify key scenes, emotions, and themes. This helps in organizing and categorizing footage for easier editing and production.

Special Effects

- **Visual Effects (VFX)**: AI is used to create and enhance visual effects in movies and TV shows. Machine learning algorithms can generate realistic animations, simulate natural phenomena, and enhance CGI.

- **Motion Capture**: AI-powered motion capture systems track and analyze human movements, allowing for the creation of realistic character animations. These systems are used in film production and video games.

AI in Education

AI is transforming education by personalizing learning experiences, improving administrative processes, and enhancing educational outcomes. This section explores the key applications of AI in education.

Personalized Learning

AI enables personalized learning experiences tailored to individual students' needs and abilities.

Adaptive Learning Platforms

- **Tailored Content**: AI-powered adaptive learning platforms adjust the content and pace of instruction based on students' performance and learning styles. These platforms provide personalized feedback and support, helping students master concepts at their own pace.

- **Intelligent Tutoring Systems**: AI-driven tutoring systems provide personalized assistance to students, identifying areas where they need improvement and offering targeted exercises and explanations.

Learning Analytics

- **Performance Tracking**: AI analyzes students' performance data to identify strengths, weaknesses, and learning patterns. This information is used to provide personalized feedback and support.

- **Predictive Analytics**: AI models predict students' future performance and identify those at risk of falling behind. Educators can use this information to intervene early and provide additional support.

Administrative Efficiency

AI is streamlining administrative processes in educational institutions, improving efficiency and reducing administrative burdens.

Enrollment and Admissions

- **Application Processing**: AI automates the processing of applications, evaluating candidates based on predefined criteria. This speeds up the admissions process and ensures consistency in decision-making.

- **Predictive Enrollment**: AI models predict enrollment trends and help institutions plan resources and staffing needs. This ensures that institutions can accommodate incoming students effectively.

Scheduling and Resource Management

- **Timetable Optimization**: AI algorithms optimize class schedules, taking into account factors such as room availability, instructor preferences, and student needs. This reduces scheduling conflicts and maximizes resource utilization.
- **Facility Management**: AI-powered systems monitor and manage campus facilities, optimizing energy usage and maintenance schedules. This reduces operational costs and improves the campus environment.

Enhanced Learning Experiences

AI is enhancing learning experiences through interactive and engaging educational tools.

Virtual Classrooms

- **AI-Powered Learning Assistants**: Virtual learning assistants, powered by AI, support students in online classrooms by answering questions, providing resources, and facilitating discussions. These assistants enhance the learning experience and provide immediate assistance.
- **Interactive Content**: AI creates interactive and immersive educational content, such as virtual labs, simulations, and educational games. These tools engage students and enhance their understanding of complex concepts.

Language Learning

- **Language Translation and Interpretation**: AI-powered

translation tools help students learn new languages by providing real-time translations and interpretations. These tools support language learning and cultural exchange.

- **Speech Recognition and Feedback**: AI-driven language learning applications use speech recognition to analyze pronunciation and provide feedback. This helps students improve their speaking skills and gain confidence in their language abilities.

Conclusion

In this chapter, we have explored the diverse applications of AI across various industries, including healthcare, finance, transportation, entertainment, and education. AI is transforming these sectors by automating processes, enhancing decision-making, and creating new opportunities for innovation. As AI technology continues to evolve, its impact on different industries will only grow, driving advancements and addressing challenges in new and exciting ways. By understanding and leveraging the power of AI, organizations can unlock its full potential and achieve greater efficiency, effectiveness, and success.

CHAPTER 6: ETHICS AND CHALLENGES IN AI

The rapid advancement of artificial intelligence (AI) has brought about significant benefits across various sectors. However, these advancements also come with ethical concerns and challenges that need to be addressed to ensure the responsible development and deployment of AI technologies. In this chapter, we will explore the ethical considerations, issues of bias and fairness, privacy and security concerns, and the potential impact of AI on employment and the future of work.

Ethical Considerations

Ethical considerations in AI encompass a wide range of issues, from the moral implications of AI decisions to the responsibility of developers and organizations in ensuring ethical AI practices. Here, we will discuss some of the most pressing ethical concerns in AI.

AI and Moral Decision-Making

One of the fundamental ethical concerns is the ability of AI systems to make moral and ethical decisions.

Autonomous Systems

- **Self-Driving Cars**: Autonomous vehicles must make split-second decisions in critical situations, such as choosing between different courses of action that may result in harm. The ethical dilemma of programming these decisions raises questions about responsibility and accountability.
- **Autonomous Weapons**: The development of AI-powered weapons systems poses significant ethical challenges. These systems could make life-and-death decisions without human intervention, raising concerns about the potential for misuse and the lack of accountability.

AI in Healthcare

- **Medical Decision-Making**: AI systems used in healthcare can influence treatment decisions, diagnoses, and patient care. Ensuring that these systems make ethically sound decisions is crucial, particularly when dealing with sensitive medical information and patient outcomes.

Transparency and Accountability

Transparency and accountability are essential for building trust in AI systems and ensuring they operate ethically.

Explainability

- **Black Box Models**: Many AI models, particularly deep learning models, are often described as "black boxes" because their decision-making processes are not easily interpretable. This lack of explainability can be problematic, especially in critical applications like finance, healthcare, and criminal justice.

- **Interpretable Models**: Developing AI models that provide clear explanations for their decisions is important for ensuring accountability and building trust with users. Techniques like LIME (Local Interpretable Model-agnostic Explanations) and SHAP (SHapley Additive exPlanations) are being developed to improve model interpretability.

Responsibility and Liability

- **Developer Responsibility**: AI developers and organizations must ensure that their systems are designed and implemented ethically. This includes conducting thorough testing, addressing potential biases, and considering the broader societal impact of their AI technologies.

- **Legal and Regulatory Frameworks**: Governments and regulatory bodies are working to establish legal frameworks that define the responsibility and liability of AI systems. These frameworks aim to ensure that AI technologies are developed and deployed responsibly and that there are mechanisms for accountability in case of harm or misuse.

Human Rights and AI

AI technologies have the potential to impact fundamental human rights, including privacy, freedom of expression, and equality.

Privacy

- **Data Collection and Surveillance**: AI systems often rely on large amounts of data, raising concerns about privacy and surveillance. The collection and use of personal data must be done transparently and with the consent of individuals.

- **Data Protection Regulations**: Laws like the General Data Protection Regulation (GDPR) in the European Union aim to protect individuals' privacy by regulating data collection, processing, and storage. Compliance with these regulations is essential for ensuring that AI systems respect individuals' privacy rights.

Freedom of Expression

- **Content Moderation**: AI is increasingly used for content moderation on social media platforms. While AI can help identify and remove harmful content, it also raises concerns about censorship and the suppression of free speech. Ensuring that content moderation policies are fair and transparent is crucial for protecting freedom of expression.

- **Deepfakes and Misinformation**: AI-generated deepfakes and misinformation can manipulate public opinion and undermine trust in information sources. Addressing these challenges requires a balance between protecting free speech and preventing the spread of harmful content.

Equality and Non-Discrimination

- **Bias in AI Systems**: AI systems can perpetuate and even exacerbate existing biases and inequalities if not carefully designed and tested. Ensuring that AI technologies are fair and unbiased is crucial for promoting equality and preventing discrimination.

- **Inclusive AI Development**: Involving diverse teams in AI development and considering the needs of different communities can help ensure that AI systems are designed to be inclusive and equitable.

Bias and Fairness in AI

Bias in AI systems is a significant concern, as it can lead to unfair and discriminatory outcomes. Addressing bias and ensuring fairness in AI is essential for building trustworthy and ethical AI technologies.

Sources of Bias

Bias in AI can arise from various sources, including data, algorithms, and human decision-making.

Data Bias

- **Historical Bias**: AI systems trained on historical data can inherit biases present in that data. For example, if historical hiring data reflects gender or racial biases, an AI system trained on that data may perpetuate those biases in its recommendations.
- **Sampling Bias**: Bias can also occur if the training data is not representative of the population. For example, an AI system trained on data from one demographic group may not perform well for other groups.

Algorithmic Bias

- **Design Bias**: Bias can be introduced during the design and development of AI algorithms. For example, if certain features are given more importance than others, it can lead to biased outcomes.
- **Model Training**: The training process itself can introduce

bias, particularly if the model is not properly validated and tested on diverse datasets.

Human Bias

- **Human Influence**: Bias can be introduced by the human developers and data scientists involved in designing and training AI systems. Their own biases and assumptions can influence the decisions made during the development process.

Addressing Bias

Addressing bias in AI requires a multifaceted approach that involves careful data management, algorithmic design, and ongoing monitoring.

Data Management

- **Diverse Datasets**: Ensuring that training datasets are diverse and representative of the population is crucial for minimizing bias. This includes collecting data from different demographic groups and considering various perspectives.
- **Data Preprocessing**: Techniques like data augmentation, resampling, and debiasing can help address biases in the training data. Data preprocessing should aim to create balanced and fair datasets.

Algorithmic Design

- **Fairness Constraints**: Incorporating fairness constraints into the algorithmic design can help ensure that the AI system produces equitable outcomes. Techniques like adversarial debiasing and fairness-aware learning can be used to mitigate bias.

- **Regular Audits**: Regularly auditing AI systems for bias and fairness is essential for identifying and addressing potential issues. This includes testing the system on diverse datasets and evaluating its performance across different demographic groups.

Human Oversight

- **Ethical Review Boards**: Establishing ethical review boards to oversee AI development and deployment can help ensure that ethical considerations are taken into account. These boards can provide guidance on addressing bias and ensuring fairness.

- **Diverse Development Teams**: Involving diverse teams in AI development can help identify and address biases that may be overlooked by homogenous groups. Diversity in perspectives and experiences can lead to more inclusive and fair AI systems.

Privacy and Security Concerns

AI systems often require large amounts of data, raising concerns about privacy and security. Ensuring that AI technologies are designed and implemented with privacy and security in mind is crucial for building trust and protecting individuals' rights.

Privacy Concerns

Privacy concerns in AI revolve around the collection, storage, and use of personal data.

Data Collection

- **Informed Consent**: Individuals should be informed about the data being collected, how it will be used, and who will have access to it. Obtaining informed consent is essential for respecting individuals' privacy rights.

- **Minimization**: Collecting only the data that is necessary for the specific purpose and minimizing data retention can help reduce privacy risks.

Data Storage

- **Encryption**: Encrypting data both at rest and in transit is essential for protecting it from unauthorized access. Strong encryption practices ensure that data remains secure even if it is intercepted.

- **Access Controls**: Implementing strict access controls to limit who can access the data is crucial for protecting privacy. This includes using authentication and authorization mechanisms to ensure that only authorized individuals can access sensitive data.

Data Use

- **Anonymization**: Anonymizing data can help protect individuals' privacy by removing personally identifiable information. However, it is important to ensure that anonymization techniques are robust and cannot be easily reversed.

- **Purpose Limitation**: Data should be used only for the purposes for which it was collected. Repurposing data without individuals' consent can violate privacy rights and erode trust.

Security Concerns

Security concerns in AI include protecting AI systems from

cyberattacks, ensuring the integrity of data, and preventing misuse of AI technologies.

Cybersecurity

- **Vulnerability Assessment**: Regularly assessing AI systems for vulnerabilities and addressing any identified issues is crucial for maintaining security. This includes testing for potential attack vectors and implementing security patches.
- **Adversarial Attacks**: AI systems can be vulnerable to adversarial attacks, where malicious inputs are designed to deceive the system. Techniques like adversarial training and robust optimization can help defend against these attacks.

Data Integrity

- **Data Quality**: Ensuring the quality and integrity of the data used to train AI systems is essential for preventing biases and errors. This includes validating data sources, cleaning data, and monitoring for data drift.
- **Tamper-Resistant Data**: Implementing measures to protect data from tampering, such as using cryptographic techniques and secure logging, can help ensure data integrity.

Misuse of AI

- **Ethical Guidelines**: Developing and adhering to ethical guidelines for the use of AI technologies can help prevent misuse. These guidelines should outline acceptable and unacceptable uses of AI and provide a framework for ethical decision-making.
- **Regulatory Compliance

**: Ensuring compliance with relevant laws and regulations, such as data protection and anti-discrimination laws, is crucial for preventing misuse of AI technologies. Organizations should stay informed about legal requirements and implement measures to comply with them.

Impact on Employment and the Future of Work

The rise of AI has significant implications for employment and the future of work. While AI has the potential to create new opportunities and improve productivity, it also raises concerns about job displacement and the need for workforce reskilling.

Job Displacement

AI and automation technologies have the potential to displace certain jobs, particularly those that involve routine and repetitive tasks.

Automation of Routine Tasks

- **Manufacturing**: AI-powered robots and automation systems are increasingly being used in manufacturing to perform tasks such as assembly, welding, and quality control. While this improves efficiency, it also reduces the demand for manual labor.

- **Administrative Tasks**: AI systems can automate routine administrative tasks, such as data entry, scheduling, and customer support. This can lead to job displacement in roles that involve these tasks.

Impact on Different Sectors

- **Retail**: AI technologies, such as automated checkout systems and inventory management, are transforming the retail sector. While these innovations improve efficiency, they can also reduce the need for retail workers.

- **Transportation**: Autonomous vehicles and AI-powered logistics systems have the potential to disrupt the transportation industry. Jobs in driving, delivery, and logistics may be affected as these technologies become more widespread.

Workforce Reskilling

As AI transforms the job market, there is a growing need for workforce reskilling to help individuals adapt to new roles and opportunities.

Upskilling and Reskilling Programs

- **Training Programs**: Governments, educational institutions, and businesses are investing in upskilling and reskilling programs to help workers develop new skills. These programs focus on areas such as digital literacy, data analysis, and AI technology.

- **Online Learning Platforms**: Online learning platforms, such as Coursera, edX, and Udacity, offer courses and certifications in AI, machine learning, and other emerging technologies. These platforms provide accessible and flexible learning opportunities for individuals seeking to update their skills.

Lifelong Learning

- **Continuous Learning**: The rapid pace of technological change requires a shift towards lifelong learning. Workers must continuously update their skills and knowledge to remain competitive in the job market.

- **Employer Support**: Employers can support lifelong learning by providing opportunities for training and development, offering tuition assistance, and creating a culture of continuous improvement.

New Opportunities and Job Creation

While AI may displace certain jobs, it also has the potential to create new opportunities and roles.

Emerging Job Roles

- **AI and Data Specialists**: The demand for AI and data specialists is growing as organizations seek to leverage AI technologies. Roles such as data scientists, machine learning engineers, and AI ethicists are becoming increasingly important.
- **Tech-Enhanced Roles**: AI can augment existing roles, enabling workers to perform tasks more efficiently and effectively. For example, AI-powered tools can assist doctors in diagnosing diseases, teachers in personalizing instruction, and marketers in analyzing consumer behavior.

Innovation and Entrepreneurship

- **Startups and Innovation**: AI is driving innovation and entrepreneurship, with new startups emerging to develop AI-powered solutions across various industries. This creates opportunities for entrepreneurs and fosters economic growth.
- **Creative Industries**: AI is enabling new forms of creativity and expression in industries such as art, music,

and entertainment. AI-powered tools are being used to create original content, opening up new possibilities for artists and creators.

Summary

The ethical considerations and challenges associated with AI are complex and multifaceted. Addressing these issues requires a collaborative effort from governments, businesses, researchers, and society as a whole. By focusing on transparency, accountability, fairness, privacy, and security, we can ensure the responsible development and deployment of AI technologies. Moreover, as AI continues to transform the job market, it is essential to invest in workforce reskilling and create new opportunities for individuals to thrive in the evolving landscape. By navigating these ethical and practical challenges, we can harness the full potential of AI to benefit society while mitigating its risks.

CHAPTER 7: GETTING STARTED WITH AI PROGRAMMING

Artificial intelligence (AI) programming can seem daunting for beginners, but with the right resources and guidance, anyone can start learning and building AI models. This chapter will provide a comprehensive guide to getting started with AI programming, including an introduction to Python for AI, basic AI programming exercises, and a step-by-step guide to building your first AI project.

Introduction to Python for AI

Python is the most popular programming language for AI and machine learning due to its simplicity, readability, and extensive library support. This section will introduce the basics of Python and some essential libraries for AI programming.

Why Python for AI?

Python is the preferred language for AI and machine learning for several reasons:

- **Ease of Learning**: Python's syntax is straightforward and readable, making it accessible for beginners.

- **Extensive Libraries**: Python has a rich ecosystem of libraries and frameworks for AI and machine learning, such as TensorFlow, PyTorch, Keras, Scikit-Learn, and more.

- **Community Support**: Python has a large and active community, providing ample resources, tutorials, and forums for support.

- **Integration**: Python integrates well with other languages and tools, making it versatile for various applications.

Setting Up Your Python Environment

To get started with Python for AI, you'll need to set up your development environment. Here's a step-by-step guide to setting up Python and essential libraries.

Installing Python

1. **Download and Install Python**: Visit the official [Python website](https://www.python.org/downloads/) and download the latest version of Python. Follow the installation instructions for your operating system.

2. **Verify the Installation**: Open a terminal or command prompt and run the following command to verify that Python is installed correctly:

   ```sh
   python --version
   ```

Setting Up a Virtual Environment

A virtual environment is an isolated environment that allows you to manage dependencies for your Python projects.

1. **Create a Virtual Environment**: Run the following command to create a virtual environment:

   ```sh
   python -m venv myenv
   ```

   Replace `myenv` with the name of your virtual environment.

2. **Activate the Virtual Environment**: Activate the virtual environment using the following command:

   - On Windows:

     ```sh
     myenv\Scripts\activate
     ```

   - On macOS and Linux:

     ```sh
     source myenv/bin/activate
     ```

3. **Deactivate the Virtual Environment**: To deactivate the virtual environment, simply run:

```sh
deactivate
```

Installing Essential Libraries

Once your virtual environment is set up, you can install the essential libraries for AI programming. Here are some key libraries and their installation commands:

- **NumPy**: A library for numerical computing.

    ```sh
    pip install numpy
    ```

- **Pandas**: A library for data manipulation and analysis.

    ```sh
    pip install pandas
    ```

- **Matplotlib**: A library for data visualization.

    ```sh
    pip install matplotlib
    ```

- **Scikit-Learn**: A library for machine learning.

```sh
pip install scikit-learn
```

- **TensorFlow**: A library for deep learning.

    ```sh
    pip install tensorflow
    ```

- **PyTorch**: Another popular library for deep learning.

    ```sh
    pip install torch torchvision
    ```

- **Keras**: A high-level API for building and training deep learning models.

    ```sh
    pip install keras
    ```

Basic Python Programming Concepts

Before diving into AI programming, it's important to understand some basic Python programming concepts. This section will cover variables, data types, control structures, functions, and classes.

Variables and Data Types

Variables are used to store data in Python. Here are some common data types:

- **Integers**: Whole numbers.

    ```python
    age = 25
    ```

- **Floats**: Decimal numbers.

    ```python
    temperature = 98.6
    ```

- **Strings**: Text data.

    ```python
    name = "Alice"
    ```

- **Lists**: Ordered collections of items.

    ```python
    fruits = ["apple", "banana", "cherry"]
    ```

- **Dictionaries**: Collections of key-value pairs.

    ```python
    student = {"name": "Alice", "age": 25, "grade": "A"}
    ```

Control Structures

Control structures are used to control the flow of a program.

- **If Statements**: Conditional statements.

    ```python
    if age >= 18:
        print("Adult")
    else:
        print("Minor")
    ```

- **For Loops**: Iterating over a sequence.

    ```python
    for fruit in fruits:
        print(fruit)
    ```

- **While Loops**: Repeating a block of code while a condition is true.

```python
count = 0
while count < 5:
    print(count)
    count += 1
```

Functions

Functions are reusable blocks of code that perform a specific task.

- **Defining a Function**:

```python
def greet(name):
    return f"Hello, {name}!"
```

- **Calling a Function**:

```python
message = greet("Alice")
print(message)
```

Classes and Objects

Classes are blueprints for creating objects (instances of the class).

- **Defining a Class**:

    ```python
    class Dog:
        def __init__(self, name, age):
            self.name = name
            self.age = age

        def bark(self):
            return f"{self.name} says woof!"
    ```

- **Creating an Object**:

    ```python
    my_dog = Dog("Buddy", 3)
    print(my_dog.bark())
    ```

Basic AI Programming Exercises

To get hands-on experience with AI programming, let's start with some basic exercises. These exercises will introduce you to data manipulation, machine learning, and neural networks using Python.

Exercise 1: Data Manipulation with Pandas

Pandas is a powerful library for data manipulation and analysis. In this exercise, we will load a dataset, perform some basic data manipulation, and visualize the data.

Step-by-Step Guide

1. **Load the Dataset**: We will use the Iris dataset, which is a common dataset in machine learning.

    ```python
    import pandas as pd

    # Load the Iris dataset
    url = "https://archive.ics.uci.edu/ml/machine-learning-databases/iris/iris.data"
    column_names = ["sepal_length", "sepal_width", "petal_length", "petal_width", "class"]
    iris = pd.read_csv(url, header=None, names=column_names)
    ```

2. **Explore the Dataset**: Get an overview of the dataset.

    ```python
    # Display the first few rows of the dataset
    print(iris.head())

    # Display basic statistics of the dataset
    print(iris.describe())

    # Display the distribution of the classes
```

```python
print(iris["class"].value_counts())
```

3. **Data Visualization**: Use Matplotlib to create a scatter plot of the data.

```python
import matplotlib.pyplot as plt

# Scatter plot of sepal length vs. sepal width
plt.scatter(iris["sepal_length"], iris["sepal_width"], c=iris["class"].astype("category").cat.codes)
plt.xlabel("Sepal Length")
plt.ylabel("Sepal Width")
plt.title("Sepal Length vs. Sepal Width")
plt.show()
```

Exercise 2: Machine Learning with Scikit-Learn

Scikit-Learn is a popular library for machine learning in Python. In this exercise, we will build a simple machine learning model to classify the Iris dataset.

Step-by-Step Guide

1. **Load the Dataset**: We will use the same Iris dataset from the previous exercise.

```python
```

```python
import pandas as pd
from sklearn.model_selection import train_test_split
from sklearn.preprocessing import StandardScaler
from sklearn.linear_model import LogisticRegression
from sklearn.metrics import accuracy_score

# Load the Iris dataset
url = "https://archive.ics.uci.edu/ml/machine-learning-databases/iris/iris.data"
column_names = ["sepal_length", "sepal_width", "petal_length", "petal_width", "class"]
iris = pd.read_csv(url, header=None, names=column_names)
```

2. **Prepare the Data**: Split the data into training and testing sets, and standardize the features.

```python
# Split the data into features (X) and target (y)
X = iris.drop("class", axis=1)
y = iris["class"]

# Split the data into training and testing sets
X_train, X_test, y_train, y_test = train_test_split(X, y, test_size=0.2, random_state=42)

# Standardize the features
scaler = StandardScaler()
X_train = scaler.fit_transform(X_train)
```

```
X_test = scaler.transform(X_test)
```

3. **Train the Model**: Train a logistic regression model on the training data.

```python
# Train a logistic regression model
model = LogisticRegression()
model.fit(X_train, y_train)
```

4. **Evaluate the Model**: Evaluate the model's performance on the testing data.

```python
# Make predictions on the testing data
y_pred = model.predict(X_test)

# Calculate the accuracy of the model
accuracy = accuracy_score(y_test, y_pred)
print(f"Accuracy: {accuracy}")
```

Exercise 3: Neural Networks with TensorFlow and Keras

TensorFlow and Keras are powerful libraries for building and training neural networks. In this exercise, we will build a simple neural network to classify the MNIST dataset.

Step-by-Step Guide

1. **Load the Dataset**: We will use the MNIST dataset, which contains images of handwritten digits.

```python
import tensorflow as tf
from tensorflow.keras import layers, models

# Load the MNIST dataset
(train_images, train_labels), (test_images, test_labels) = tf.keras.datasets.mnist.load_data()
```

2. **Preprocess the Data**: Normalize the image data and reshape it for the neural network.

```python
# Normalize the image data
train_images = train_images / 255.0
test_images = test_images / 255.0

# Reshape the image data
train_images = train_images.reshape((train_images.shape[0], 28, 28, 1))
test_images = test_images.reshape((test_images.shape[0], 28, 28, 1))
```

3. **Build the Model**: Define the architecture of the neural network.

```python
# Build the neural network model
model = models.Sequential([
    layers.Conv2D(32, (3, 3), activation="relu", input_shape=(28, 28, 1)),
    layers.MaxPooling2D((2, 2)),
    layers.Conv2D(64, (3, 3), activation="relu"),
    layers.MaxPooling2D((2, 2)),
    layers.Conv2D(64, (3, 3), activation="relu"),
    layers.Flatten(),
    layers.Dense(64, activation="relu"),
    layers.Dense(10, activation="softmax")
])
```

4. **Compile the Model**: Configure the model for training.

```python
# Compile the model
model.compile(optimizer="adam",
              loss="sparse_categorical_crossentropy",
              metrics=["accuracy"])
```

5. **Train the Model**: Train the neural network on the training

data.

```python
# Train the model
model.fit(train_images, train_labels, epochs=5, batch_size=64)
```

6. **Evaluate the Model**: Evaluate the model's performance on the testing data.

```python
# Evaluate the model
test_loss, test_acc = model.evaluate(test_images, test_labels)
print(f"Test accuracy: {test_acc}")
```

Building Your First AI Project

Building a complete AI project involves several steps, including data collection, preprocessing, model building, training, evaluation, and deployment. In this section, we will guide you through the process of building your first AI project from start to finish.

Project Overview

For this project, we will build a machine learning model to predict house prices using the California Housing dataset. The dataset contains information about various features of houses and their corresponding prices.

Step 1: Data Collection

First, we need to collect and load the dataset. The California Housing dataset is available in Scikit-Learn.

```python
import pandas as pd
from sklearn.datasets import fetch_california_housing

# Load the California Housing dataset
data = fetch_california_housing()
housing = pd.DataFrame(data.data, columns=data.feature_names)
housing["target"] = data.target

# Display the first few rows of the dataset
print(housing.head())
```

Step 2: Data Preprocessing

Next, we need to preprocess the data to make it suitable for training a machine learning model. This includes handling missing values, encoding categorical features, and scaling numerical features.

```python
from sklearn.model_selection import train_test_split
from sklearn.preprocessing import StandardScaler
```

```
# Split the data into features (X) and target (y)
X = housing.drop("target", axis=1)
y = housing["target"]

# Split the data into training and testing sets
X_train, X_test, y_train, y_test = train_test_split(X, y, test_size=0.2, random_state=42)

# Standardize the features
scaler = StandardScaler()
X_train = scaler.fit_transform(X_train)
X_test = scaler.transform(X_test)
```

Step 3: Model Building

We will build a simple regression model using Scikit-Learn's LinearRegression algorithm.

```python
from sklearn.linear_model import LinearRegression

# Build the regression model
model = LinearRegression()
```

Step 4: Model Training

Train the model on the training data.

```python
# Train the model
model.fit(X_train, y_train)
```

Step 5: Model Evaluation

Evaluate the model's performance on the testing data.

```python
from sklearn.metrics import mean_squared_error

# Make predictions on the testing data
y_pred = model.predict(X_test)

# Calculate the mean squared error
mse = mean_squared_error(y_test, y_pred)
print(f"Mean Squared Error: {mse}")
```

Step 6: Model Deployment

Deploying an AI model involves making it accessible for use in a production environment. For simplicity, we will demonstrate how to save and load the model using joblib.

```python
import joblib
```

```
# Save the model to a file
joblib.dump(model, "house_price_model.pkl")

# Load the model from the file
loaded_model = joblib.load("house_price_model.pkl")

# Make predictions using the loaded model
y_loaded_pred = loaded_model.predict(X_test)
print(f"Loaded Model Mean Squared Error: {mean_squared_error(y_test, y_loaded_pred)}")
```

Summary

In this chapter, we have introduced the basics of AI programming, including an introduction to Python for AI, basic programming exercises, and a step-by-step guide to building your first AI project. By following these steps and practicing with the exercises, you can gain hands-on experience and build a solid foundation in AI programming. As you continue your journey in AI, remember to explore more advanced topics, experiment with different algorithms, and stay updated with the latest developments in the field.

CHAPTER 8: FUTURE TRENDS IN AI

Artificial Intelligence (AI) is an ever-evolving field that continues to make significant strides in technology, society, and industry. The future holds even more promise as new trends and innovations emerge. In this chapter, we will explore the future trends in AI, including emerging AI technologies, AI and the Internet of Things (IoT), AI in augmented and virtual reality (AR/VR), and predictions for the future of AI.

Emerging AI Technologies

AI technologies are continuously advancing, leading to the development of new tools, techniques, and applications. This section highlights some of the most promising emerging AI technologies.

Explainable AI (XAI)

Explainable AI (XAI) aims to make AI systems more transparent, understandable, and trustworthy. Traditional AI models, especially deep learning models, often function as "black boxes" with little insight into their decision-making processes. XAI seeks to address this issue.

Key Concepts

- **Model Interpretability**: XAI focuses on creating models that provide clear and understandable explanations for their decisions. Techniques such as LIME (Local Interpretable Model-agnostic Explanations) and SHAP (SHapley Additive exPlanations) help interpret complex models.
- **Transparency**: Ensuring that AI systems are transparent about how they operate and make decisions is crucial for building trust and accountability.
- **User Trust**: By providing explanations for AI decisions, XAI helps users trust and understand AI systems, leading to better adoption and acceptance.

Applications

- **Healthcare**: In medical diagnostics, XAI can help healthcare professionals understand the reasoning behind AI-driven diagnoses and treatment recommendations, improving patient care.
- **Finance**: In financial services, XAI can provide transparency in credit scoring, fraud detection, and investment decisions, ensuring fairness and accountability.

Fedcrated Learning

Federated learning is a distributed machine learning approach that allows models to be trained across multiple decentralized devices or servers without sharing raw data. This approach enhances data privacy and security.

Key Concepts

- **Decentralized Training**: Instead of centralizing data,

federated learning trains models locally on each device and aggregates the results to build a global model.

- **Privacy Preservation**: By keeping data on local devices, federated learning reduces the risk of data breaches and enhances privacy.

- **Scalability**: Federated learning can scale to a large number of devices, making it suitable for applications with vast and distributed datasets.

Applications

- **Mobile Devices**: Federated learning is used in mobile devices to improve features like predictive text, voice recognition, and personalized recommendations without compromising user privacy.

- **Healthcare**: In healthcare, federated learning enables collaborative research and model training across multiple institutions while protecting patient data.

Quantum Machine Learning

Quantum machine learning combines quantum computing and machine learning to create powerful algorithms that can solve complex problems more efficiently than classical algorithms.

Key Concepts

- **Quantum Computing**: Quantum computers use quantum bits (qubits) that can represent and process information in ways that classical bits cannot, enabling parallelism and faster computations.

- **Quantum Algorithms**: Quantum machine learning leverages quantum algorithms, such as the quantum version of the k-means clustering algorithm and quantum support vector machines, to perform tasks more efficiently.

Applications

- **Optimization**: Quantum machine learning can solve optimization problems in logistics, finance, and supply chain management more efficiently than classical methods.
- **Drug Discovery**: In drug discovery, quantum machine learning can analyze complex molecular structures and interactions, accelerating the development of new drugs.

Neuromorphic Computing

Neuromorphic computing aims to mimic the structure and function of the human brain by using specialized hardware and algorithms. This approach has the potential to create more efficient and powerful AI systems.

Key Concepts

- **Brain-Inspired Architecture**: Neuromorphic systems use architectures inspired by the human brain, such as spiking neural networks, to process information.
- **Energy Efficiency**: Neuromorphic computing is designed to be energy-efficient, making it suitable for applications where power consumption is a critical factor.

Applications

- **Robotics**: Neuromorphic computing can enhance the capabilities of robots by enabling them to process sensory information and make decisions more efficiently.

- **Real-Time Processing**: In real-time applications, such as autonomous vehicles and drones, neuromorphic computing can provide faster and more efficient processing.

AI and the Internet of Things (IoT)

The integration of AI and IoT is creating intelligent systems that can collect, analyze, and act on data in real time. This section explores how AI is enhancing IoT applications and the impact of this integration.

Key Concepts

- **Smart Devices**: IoT devices equipped with sensors and connectivity can collect vast amounts of data from their environment.
- **Edge Computing**: AI algorithms can be deployed on edge devices, allowing data to be processed locally, reducing latency, and improving efficiency.
- **Data Analytics**: AI enables advanced data analytics, allowing IoT systems to gain insights and make intelligent decisions based on real-time data.

Applications

Smart Homes

- **Home Automation**: AI-powered IoT devices can automate various tasks in the home, such as adjusting lighting, controlling temperature, and managing security systems.
- **Voice Assistants**: Voice-activated AI assistants, such as Amazon Alexa and Google Assistant, can interact with IoT devices to provide a seamless and intelligent home experience.

Industrial IoT (IIoT)

- **Predictive Maintenance**: AI algorithms analyze data from industrial equipment to predict failures and schedule maintenance, reducing downtime and costs.

- **Quality Control**: AI-powered IoT systems can monitor production processes in real-time, detecting defects and ensuring product quality.

Smart Cities

- **Traffic Management**: AI and IoT systems can monitor and manage traffic flow, reducing congestion and improving transportation efficiency.

- **Energy Management**: AI algorithms optimize energy consumption in smart grids, buildings, and infrastructure, promoting sustainability and reducing costs.

Challenges

- **Data Privacy**: The integration of AI and IoT raises concerns about data privacy and security. Ensuring that data is collected, processed, and stored securely is crucial.

- **Interoperability**: Ensuring that different IoT devices and systems can communicate and work together seamlessly is a significant challenge.

- **Scalability**: Scaling AI and IoT systems to handle large volumes of data and devices requires robust infrastructure and efficient algorithms.

AI in Augmented and Virtual Reality (AR/VR)

AI is transforming augmented reality (AR) and virtual reality (VR) by enhancing user experiences, creating immersive environments, and enabling new applications. This section explores the role of AI in AR and VR and its impact on various industries.

Key Concepts

- **Augmented Reality (AR)**: AR overlays digital information, such as images, videos, and data, onto the real world, enhancing the user's perception and interaction with their environment.
- **Virtual Reality (VR)**: VR creates immersive, computer-generated environments that simulate real or imagined worlds, allowing users to interact with them in a seemingly real way.
- **Mixed Reality (MR)**: MR combines elements of both AR and VR, blending digital and physical worlds to create interactive and immersive experiences.

Applications

Gaming and Entertainment

- **Immersive Experiences**: AI enhances AR and VR gaming experiences by creating realistic environments, intelligent NPCs (non-player characters), and dynamic storylines.
- **Personalization**: AI algorithms analyze player behavior and preferences to personalize gaming experiences, making them more engaging and enjoyable.

Education and Training

- **Interactive Learning**: AI-powered AR and VR applications provide interactive and immersive learning experiences, helping students understand complex concepts through visualization and simulation.

- **Virtual Training**: In industries such as healthcare, aviation, and manufacturing, AI-driven VR training programs simulate real-world scenarios, allowing trainees to practice skills and decision-making in a safe environment.

Healthcare

- **Surgical Training**: VR and AI technologies enable surgeons to practice procedures in a simulated environment, improving their skills and reducing the risk of errors.
- **Therapeutic Applications**: AR and VR, combined with AI, are used in therapeutic applications such as pain management, physical therapy, and mental health treatment.

Retail and E-Commerce

- **Virtual Try-Ons**: AI-powered AR applications allow customers to virtually try on clothing, accessories, and makeup, enhancing the shopping experience and reducing returns.
- **Immersive Shopping**: VR creates immersive shopping environments where customers can explore virtual stores and interact with products in a realistic way.

Challenges

- **Hardware Limitations**: The performance and resolution of AR and VR devices can impact the quality of user experiences. Advancements in hardware are needed to create more realistic and immersive environments.
- **Content Creation**: Developing high-quality AR and VR

content requires significant time, effort, and expertise. AI can help automate and enhance content creation, but challenges remain.

- **User Adoption**: Widespread adoption of AR and VR technologies depends on user acceptance and the availability of affordable, user-friendly devices.

Predictions for the Future of AI

As AI continues to evolve, its impact on society, industry, and technology will grow. This section explores predictions for the future of AI and its potential implications.

AI and Human Collaboration

AI and humans will increasingly collaborate, leveraging each other's strengths to achieve better outcomes.

Augmented Intelligence

- **Human-AI Teams**: AI will assist humans in various tasks, providing data-driven insights, recommendations, and support. Human-AI teams will be more effective and efficient than either working alone.

- **Decision Support**: AI will enhance human decision-making by analyzing large volumes of data, identifying patterns, and providing actionable insights.

AI in Everyday Life

AI will become an integral part of everyday life, enhancing convenience, productivity, and quality of life.

Smart Assistants

- **Voice Assistants**: AI-powered voice assistants will become more advanced, understanding natural language and context more accurately, and providing more useful and personalized responses.
- **Personal Assistants**: AI will help manage daily tasks, such as scheduling, reminders, and information retrieval, making life more organized and efficient.

Healthcare

- **Personalized Medicine**: AI will enable more precise and personalized medical treatments, improving patient outcomes and reducing healthcare costs.
- **Preventive Healthcare**: AI-powered wearables and health monitoring devices will provide real-time health data, enabling early detection and prevention of diseases.

AI and the Workforce

AI will transform the workforce, creating new job roles and changing the nature of work.

Job Transformation

- **Reskilling and Upskilling**: Workers will need to acquire new skills to adapt to the changing job market. Lifelong learning and continuous education will become essential.
- **New Job Roles**: AI will create new job roles in areas such as

AI ethics, data analysis, and AI system management, providing opportunities for career growth and development.

Ethical and Regulatory Considerations

The ethical and regulatory landscape for AI will evolve to address new challenges and ensure responsible AI development and deployment.

Ethical AI

- **Fairness and Bias**: Efforts to ensure fairness and reduce bias in AI systems will continue to be a priority, with advancements in techniques and best practices.
- **Transparency and Accountability**: Regulatory frameworks will mandate transparency and accountability in AI systems, requiring explainability and clear guidelines for AI deployment.

Data Privacy and Security

- **Privacy Protection**: Stronger data privacy regulations and practices will be implemented to protect individuals' data and ensure ethical data usage.
- **Cybersecurity**: AI-driven cybersecurity measures will be developed to protect against increasingly sophisticated cyber threats.

Global Collaboration and Impact

Global collaboration will be essential for addressing the challenges and maximizing the benefits of AI.

International Cooperation

- **Standards and Regulations**: International cooperation will be necessary to establish global standards and regulations for AI development and deployment.
- **Collaborative Research**: Collaborative research initiatives will drive innovation and address global challenges, such as climate change, healthcare, and sustainable development.

AI and Society

The impact of AI on society will be profound, shaping how we live, work, and interact.

Social Impact

- **Inclusion and Accessibility**: AI will be leveraged to create more inclusive and accessible technologies, improving the quality of life for people with disabilities and marginalized communities.
- **Public Awareness**: Increasing public awareness and education about AI will be essential for informed decision-making and acceptance of AI technologies.

Future Challenges

- **Ethical Dilemmas**: As AI becomes more integrated into society, new ethical dilemmas will arise, requiring ongoing dialogue and ethical considerations.
- **Balancing Benefits and Risks**: Striking a balance between the benefits and risks of AI will be crucial for ensuring that AI technologies are developed and used for the greater good.

Summary

The future of AI is filled with exciting possibilities and challenges. Emerging technologies like explainable AI, federated learning, quantum machine learning, and neuromorphic computing are pushing the boundaries of what AI can achieve. The integration of AI with IoT and AR/VR is creating intelligent, immersive, and interactive experiences that are transforming industries and everyday life. As AI continues to evolve, it will play a crucial role in shaping the future, enhancing human capabilities, and addressing global challenges. By understanding these trends and preparing for the future, we can harness the power of AI to create a better, more equitable, and sustainable world.

CHAPTER 9: RESOURCES FOR FURTHER LEARNING

Artificial Intelligence (AI) is a vast and rapidly evolving field, and continuous learning is essential for staying up-to-date with the latest advancements and trends. This chapter provides a comprehensive list of resources for further learning, including recommended books and articles, online courses and tutorials, and AI communities and conferences.

Recommended Books and Articles

Books and articles are valuable resources for gaining in-depth knowledge and insights into AI concepts, techniques, and applications. Here are some highly recommended books and articles for learners at various levels.

Books

For Beginners

1. **"Artificial Intelligence: A Guide for Thinking Humans" by Melanie Mitchell**

    - This book provides an accessible introduction to AI, covering its history, current state, and future prospects. It explores key concepts and challenges in a way that is engaging and easy to understand.

2. **"Python Machine Learning" by Sebastian Raschka and Vahid Mirjalili**

- A hands-on guide to machine learning with Python, this book covers fundamental concepts and practical implementations using popular libraries such as Scikit-Learn and TensorFlow.

3. **"Deep Learning for Beginners: An Introduction" by Dr. Pablo Rivas**

- This book offers a beginner-friendly introduction to deep learning, covering essential topics such as neural networks, backpropagation, and common architectures like CNNs and RNNs.

For Intermediate Learners

1. **"Deep Learning" by Ian Goodfellow, Yoshua Bengio, and Aaron Courville**

- A comprehensive textbook on deep learning, this book covers the theory and practice of deep learning, including neural networks, optimization, and deep generative models.

2. **"Pattern Recognition and Machine Learning" by Christopher M. Bishop**

- This book provides an in-depth exploration of machine learning and pattern recognition, covering probabilistic graphical models, Bayesian networks, and various machine learning algorithms.

3. **"Hands-On Machine Learning with Scikit-Learn, Keras, and TensorFlow" by Aurélien Géron**

   - A practical guide to machine learning, this book covers a wide range of topics, including supervised and unsupervised learning, deep learning, and reinforcement learning, with hands-on examples using Python.

For Advanced Learners

1. **"Artificial Intelligence: A Modern Approach" by Stuart Russell and Peter Norvig**

   - A seminal textbook in the field of AI, this book covers a wide range of topics, including search algorithms, knowledge representation, planning, and machine learning. It is suitable for advanced learners and practitioners.

2. **"Reinforcement Learning: An Introduction" by Richard S. Sutton and Andrew G. Barto**

   - A comprehensive introduction to reinforcement learning, this book covers fundamental concepts, algorithms, and applications, including value functions, policy gradients, and deep reinforcement learning.

3. **"Probabilistic Graphical Models: Principles and Techniques" by Daphne Koller and Nir Friedman**

   - This book provides an in-depth exploration of probabilistic graphical models, covering concepts such as Bayesian networks, Markov networks, and inference algorithms.

Articles and Papers

Key Articles

1. **"The Unreasonable Effectiveness of Data" by Alon Halevy, Peter Norvig, and Fernando Pereira**

   - This influential article discusses the importance of large-scale data in AI and machine learning and how it can lead to significant improvements in performance.

2. **"Building Machines That Learn and Think Like People" by Josh Tenenbaum, Charles Kemp, Thomas L. Griffiths, and Noah D. Goodman**

   - This article explores the intersection of AI and cognitive science, discussing how insights from human learning and reasoning can inform the development of AI systems.

3. **"AI Safety and Reliability" by Stuart Russell**

   - This article addresses the ethical and safety concerns associated with AI, discussing strategies for ensuring that AI systems are reliable, trustworthy, and aligned with human values.

Notable Papers

1. **"ImageNet Classification with Deep Convolutional Neural Networks" by Alex Krizhevsky, Ilya Sutskever, and Geoffrey Hinton**

   - This groundbreaking paper introduced the AlexNet architecture, which achieved state-of-the-art performance on the ImageNet dataset and sparked significant interest in deep learning.

2. **"Attention Is All You Need" by Ashish Vaswani, Noam Shazeer, Niki Parmar, Jakob Uszkoreit, Llion Jones, Aidan N. Gomez, Łukasz Kaiser, and Illia Polosukhin**

- This paper introduced the Transformer architecture, which has become the foundation for many state-of-the-art models in natural language processing (NLP), including BERT and GPT.

3. **"Mastering the Game of Go with Deep Neural Networks and Tree Search" by David Silver, Aja Huang, Chris J. Maddison, Arthur Guez, Laurent Sifre, George Van Den Driessche, Julian Schrittwieser, Ioannis Antonoglou, Veda Panneershelvam, Marc Lanctot, Sander Dieleman, Dominik Grewe, John Nham, Nal Kalchbrenner, Ivo Danihelka, Karen Simonyan, Marc Ali Eslami, Alex Graves, Koray Kavukcuoglu, Thore Graepel, and Demis Hassabis**

   - This paper describes AlphaGo, the first AI system to defeat a human professional Go player, and discusses the combination of deep learning and tree search used to achieve this milestone.

Online Courses and Tutorials

Online courses and tutorials are excellent resources for learning AI at your own pace. Here are some of the best online platforms and courses for AI education.

Online Learning Platforms

1. **Coursera**
   - Coursera offers a wide range of AI and machine learning courses from top universities and institutions. Courses are typically structured as video lectures, assignments, and quizzes, with the option to earn certificates.

2. **edX**
   - edX provides AI courses from leading universities, including MIT, Harvard, and Berkeley. Learners can access course

materials for free or pay for a verified certificate.

3. **Udacity**

   - Udacity offers nanodegree programs in AI, machine learning, and deep learning, providing hands-on projects, mentorship, and career support.

4. **Kaggle**

   - Kaggle, a platform for data science competitions, also offers free courses on various AI topics, including Python, machine learning, and deep learning.

Recommended Courses

For Beginners

1. **"AI For Everyone" by Andrew Ng (Coursera)**

   - This course provides a non-technical introduction to AI, covering key concepts, applications, and ethical considerations. It is suitable for business professionals and beginners who want to understand the impact of AI.

2. **"Machine Learning" by Andrew Ng (Coursera)**

   - A comprehensive introduction to machine learning, this course covers supervised and unsupervised learning, neural networks, and practical applications. It includes video lectures, quizzes, and programming assignments.

3. **"Introduction to TensorFlow for Artificial Intelligence, Machine Learning, and Deep Learning" by Laurence Moroney (Coursera)**

   - This course introduces TensorFlow, a popular deep learning framework, and covers the basics of building and training neural networks.

For Intermediate Learners

1. **"Deep Learning Specialization" by Andrew Ng and the DeepLearning.AI Team (Coursera)**

   - This specialization consists of five courses covering neural networks, deep learning, convolutional networks, sequence models, and more. It includes hands-on assignments using Python and TensorFlow.

2. **"Applied Data Science with Python Specialization" by the University of Michigan (Coursera)**

   - This specialization focuses on data science techniques, including machine learning, text analysis, and data visualization, using Python libraries such as Pandas, Scikit-Learn, and Matplotlib.

3. **"Advanced Machine Learning Specialization" by the National Research University Higher School of Economics (Coursera)**

   - This specialization covers advanced machine learning topics, including deep learning, reinforcement learning, and Bayesian methods. It includes practical assignments and projects.

For Advanced Learners

1. **"Reinforcement Learning Specialization" by the University of Alberta (Coursera)**

   - This specialization covers reinforcement learning theory and applications, including dynamic programming, Monte Carlo methods, and function approximation. It includes hands-on projects and assignments.

2. **"Probabilistic Graphical Models Specialization" by Stanford University (Coursera)**

   - This specialization covers probabilistic graphical models, including Bayesian networks, Markov networks, and inference algorithms. It includes theoretical and practical assignments.

3. **"Self-Driving Cars Specialization" by the University of Toronto (Coursera)**

   - This specialization covers the fundamentals of autonomous vehicles, including perception, localization, planning, and control. It includes hands-on projects and simulations.

AI Communities and Conferences

Joining AI communities and attending conferences are great ways to stay updated with the latest developments, network with professionals, and collaborate on projects. Here are some key AI communities and conferences.

AI Communities

1. **Kaggle**

   - Kaggle is a popular platform for data science and machine learning competitions. It provides a community of data scientists and AI enthusiasts who collaborate on projects, share knowledge, and participate in challenges.

2. **Reddit**

   - Reddit has several AI-related subreddits, including r/MachineLearning, r/ArtificialIntelligence, and r/learnmachinelearning, where users share articles, discuss research, and seek advice.

3. **GitHub**

   - GitHub is a platform for version control and collaboration, hosting numerous AI and machine learning projects. Contributing to open-source projects and joining discussions can help you learn and network with the AI community.

4. **Stack Overflow**

   - Stack Overflow is a popular Q&A platform for programmers.

The AI and machine learning tags are active, with experts providing answers and advice on various AI-related topics.

AI Conferences

1. **NeurIPS (Neural Information Processing Systems)**

   - NeurIPS is one of the most prestigious AI conferences, featuring cutting-edge research in machine learning, neural networks, and AI. It includes workshops, tutorials, and poster sessions.

2. **ICML (International Conference on Machine Learning)**

   - ICML is a leading conference in the field of machine learning, presenting the latest research and developments. It includes keynote talks, paper presentations, and workshops.

3. **CVPR (Conference on Computer Vision and Pattern Recognition)**

   - CVPR is a top conference in computer vision, featuring research on image and video analysis, pattern recognition, and related topics. It includes paper presentations, tutorials, and workshops.

4. **AAAI Conference on Artificial Intelligence**

   - The AAAI Conference on Artificial Intelligence covers a wide range of AI topics, including machine learning, robotics, natural language processing, and AI applications. It includes paper presentations, invited talks, and workshops.

5. **IJCAI (International Joint Conference on Artificial Intelligence)**

   - IJCAI is a major AI conference that brings together researchers from various AI subfields. It includes paper presentations, keynote talks, and workshops.

6. **ECCV (European Conference on Computer Vision)**

   - ECCV is a leading conference in computer vision, featuring research on image processing, object detection, and related topics. It includes paper presentations, tutorials, and workshops.

7. **AISTATS (Artificial Intelligence and Statistics)**

   - AISTATS focuses on the intersection of AI and statistics, presenting research on statistical learning, data analysis, and related topics. It includes paper presentations and workshops.

How to Get the Most Out of Conferences

1. **Plan Ahead**: Review the conference schedule and identify the sessions, workshops, and talks that align with your interests and goals. Plan your itinerary to make the most of your time.

2. **Network**: Take advantage of networking opportunities to connect with other attendees, researchers, and industry professionals. Attend social events, poster sessions, and

networking breaks.

3. **Participate**: Engage actively in sessions by asking questions, joining discussions, and providing feedback. Participate in workshops and tutorials to gain hands-on experience.

4. **Follow Up**: After the conference, follow up with the contacts you made and stay connected. Share your learnings and insights with your colleagues and continue the conversation.

Summary

Continuous learning is essential for staying current in the rapidly evolving field of AI. By leveraging the resources provided in this chapter, including books, articles, online courses, and community engagement, you can deepen your knowledge, enhance your skills, and stay updated with the latest developments in AI. Additionally, attending conferences and participating in AI communities will help you build a network of peers and professionals, fostering collaboration and innovation. As you continue your AI journey, remain curious, open to new ideas, and committed to lifelong learning.

CHAPTER 10: CONCLUSION

Artificial Intelligence (AI) has evolved from a niche academic discipline into a transformative technology that is reshaping industries, economies, and societies. Throughout this book, we have explored the fundamental concepts of AI, its key technologies, practical applications, ethical considerations, and future trends. In this final chapter, we will summarize the key points discussed, reflect on the impact of AI, and provide guidance for continued learning and engagement in the AI field.

Recap of Key Points

Introduction to Artificial Intelligence

- **Definition**: AI is the simulation of human intelligence processes by machines, including learning, reasoning, and self-correction.

- **History**: AI has a rich history, from early theoretical concepts to modern advancements in machine learning and deep learning.

- **Importance**: AI is crucial in today's world, driving innovations in various sectors and enhancing efficiency and decision-making.

Foundations of AI

- **Basic Concepts**: Understanding key concepts such as agents, environments, states, actions, and rewards is essential for grasping AI fundamentals.

- **Types of AI**: AI can be categorized into narrow AI (task-specific), general AI (human-like intelligence), and superintelligent AI (exceeds human intelligence).

- **Human vs. AI Intelligence**: While AI excels in data processing and specific tasks, human intelligence encompasses creativity, emotional understanding, and adaptability.

Key Technologies in AI

- **Machine Learning**: Techniques like supervised, unsupervised, and reinforcement learning enable machines to learn from data and make predictions.

- **Neural Networks and Deep Learning**: These technologies power advanced AI applications, such as image recognition and natural language processing.

- **Natural Language Processing (NLP)**: NLP allows machines to understand and generate human language, enabling applications like chatbots and language translation.

- **Computer Vision**: AI systems can interpret and analyze visual data, leading to applications in image recognition, object detection, and augmented reality.

- **Robotics**: AI enhances robotics, enabling autonomous systems that can perform complex tasks in various environments.

AI Tools and Platforms

- **Frameworks and Libraries**: Tools like TensorFlow, PyTorch, Keras, and Scikit-Learn facilitate AI development and deployment.

- **Cloud-Based AI Services**: Platforms from Google Cloud, AWS, and Microsoft Azure provide scalable solutions for training and deploying AI models.

- **Development Environment**: Setting up a proper development environment, including hardware and software requirements, is crucial for AI projects.

Applications of AI

- **Healthcare**: AI improves diagnostics, personalized medicine, and operational efficiency in healthcare.

- **Finance**: AI enhances fraud detection, risk management, customer service, and investment strategies.

- **Transportation**: AI powers autonomous vehicles, traffic management, and fleet optimization.

- **Entertainment**: AI personalizes content, enhances gaming experiences, and streamlines media production.

- **Education**: AI personalizes learning, improves administrative efficiency, and enhances educational outcomes.

Ethics and Challenges in AI

- **Ethical Considerations**: Transparency, accountability, and human rights are critical for ethical AI development.

- **Bias and Fairness**: Addressing bias and ensuring fairness in AI systems is essential for equitable outcomes.

- **Privacy and Security**: Protecting data privacy and ensuring security are crucial for building trust in AI.

- **Impact on Employment**: AI will transform the workforce, necessitating reskilling and the creation of new job roles.

Getting Started with AI Programming

- **Python for AI**: Python is the preferred language for AI due to its simplicity and extensive library support.
- **Basic Exercises**: Hands-on exercises in data manipulation, machine learning, and neural networks provide practical experience.
- **Building AI Projects**: A step-by-step guide to building AI projects, from data collection to model deployment, helps learners apply their knowledge.

Future Trends in AI

- **Emerging Technologies**: Explainable AI, federated learning, quantum machine learning, and neuromorphic computing are driving AI advancements.
- **AI and IoT**: The integration of AI and IoT is creating intelligent systems that can analyze and act on real-time data.
- **AI in AR/VR**: AI enhances augmented and virtual reality experiences, leading to new applications in gaming, education, and healthcare.
- **Predictions**: AI will continue to collaborate with humans, become more integrated into everyday life, and shape the future workforce.

Resources for Further Learning

- **Books and Articles**: A curated list of recommended books and articles for learners at various levels.
- **Online Courses and Tutorials**: Online platforms like Coursera, edX, and Udacity offer comprehensive AI courses and

tutorials.

- **Communities and Conferences**: Engaging with AI communities and attending conferences helps learners stay updated and network with professionals.

The Impact of AI

Societal Impact

AI has the potential to bring about profound societal changes. It can enhance quality of life, improve access to services, and drive economic growth. However, it also raises ethical, privacy, and security concerns that must be addressed to ensure its benefits are equitably distributed.

Positive Impacts

- **Healthcare**: AI-driven diagnostics and personalized treatment can improve patient outcomes and reduce healthcare costs.
- **Education**: AI-powered personalized learning can enhance educational outcomes and make learning more accessible.
- **Sustainability**: AI can optimize resource use, reduce waste, and support environmental conservation efforts.

Challenges

- **Ethics**: Ensuring that AI systems are developed and used ethically is crucial to avoid harm and build public trust.
- **Bias**: Addressing biases in AI systems is essential to prevent discrimination and ensure fairness.
- **Privacy**: Protecting individuals' data privacy is critical to

maintaining trust in AI technologies.

Economic Impact

AI is transforming industries, creating new business opportunities, and driving economic growth. However, it also poses challenges related to job displacement and the need for workforce reskilling.

Opportunities

- **Innovation**: AI is driving innovation across various sectors, leading to new products, services, and business models.
- **Efficiency**: AI improves operational efficiency, reducing costs and increasing productivity.

Challenges

- **Job Displacement**: AI and automation may displace certain jobs, necessitating workforce reskilling and adaptation.
- **Skills Gap**: The rapid pace of AI advancements requires continuous learning and skill development to keep up with industry demands.

Ethical and Regulatory Considerations

As AI becomes more integrated into society, ethical and regulatory considerations will become increasingly important.

Ethical AI

- **Fairness**: Ensuring that AI systems are fair and unbiased is crucial for promoting equality and preventing discrimination.

- **Transparency**: Making AI systems transparent and explainable helps build trust and accountability.

- **Accountability**: Defining clear accountability for AI actions and decisions ensures responsible AI development and use.

Regulatory Frameworks

- **Data Protection**: Regulations like the General Data Protection Regulation (GDPR) protect individuals' data privacy and set standards for data handling.

- **AI Ethics Guidelines**: Developing and adhering to ethical guidelines for AI development and deployment helps ensure that AI technologies are used responsibly.

Encouragement for Continued Learning

AI is a rapidly evolving field, and continuous learning is essential for staying current and advancing in the field. Here are some tips for continued learning and engagement in AI.

Stay Curious

- **Explore New Topics**: Continuously explore new AI topics, technologies, and applications to expand your knowledge and stay updated with industry trends.

- **Experiment**: Experiment with different AI techniques and tools to gain hands-on experience and deepen your understanding.

Engage with the Community

- **Join AI Communities**: Engage with AI communities, such as Kaggle, Reddit, and GitHub, to collaborate with peers, share knowledge, and participate in discussions.

- **Attend Conferences**: Attend AI conferences and workshops to learn from experts, network with professionals, and stay updated with the latest research and developments.

Invest in Lifelong Learning

- **Take Online Courses**: Enroll in online courses and specializations to gain structured learning and certifications in AI and related fields.

- **Read Books and Articles**: Read books and articles on AI to deepen your understanding of key concepts, techniques, and applications.

Contribute to Open Source Projects

- **Collaborate on Projects**: Contribute to open-source AI projects on platforms like GitHub to gain practical experience, improve your skills, and collaborate with other developers.

- **Share Your Work**: Share your AI projects, code, and insights with the community through blogs, GitHub repositories, and social media.

The Future of AI for Beginners

AI is a dynamic and rapidly growing field with immense potential for innovation and impact. As a beginner, you have the opportunity to contribute to this exciting field and shape its future. Here are some final thoughts and encouragement for your AI journey.

Embrace the Learning Journey

- **Start Small**: Begin with basic AI concepts and gradually build your knowledge and skills. Take advantage of the many resources available, including books, online courses, and tutorials.
- **Be Persistent**: Learning AI can be challenging, but persistence and practice are key to mastering the field. Keep experimenting, learning from mistakes, and seeking help when needed.

Make a Positive Impact

- **Ethical AI**: Strive to develop AI systems that are ethical, fair, and beneficial to society. Consider the broader implications of your work and prioritize the well-being of users and communities.
- **Innovation**: Use your skills and creativity to drive innovation and solve real-world problems. AI has the potential to address some of the most pressing challenges of our time, and your contributions can make a difference.

Build a Supportive Network

- **Mentorship**: Seek out mentors and experienced professionals who can provide guidance, support, and insights as you progress in your AI journey.
- **Collaboration**: Collaborate with peers, join AI communities, and participate in projects and competitions to learn from others and share your knowledge.

Summary

The field of artificial intelligence is vast, dynamic, and full of potential. As you embark on your AI journey, remember that continuous learning, ethical considerations, and collaboration are key to success. By staying curious, engaging with the community, and making a positive impact, you can contribute to the advancement of AI and help shape a future where AI technologies benefit society as a whole. Embrace the challenges and opportunities that come with learning AI, and look forward to a rewarding and impactful career in this exciting field.

CHAPTER 11: GLOSSARY

Artificial Intelligence (AI) is a complex field with a wide range of concepts, terms, and techniques. This glossary provides definitions and explanations for key terms and concepts in AI to help readers understand and navigate the field more effectively.

A

Algorithm

A set of rules or instructions designed to solve a problem or perform a specific task. In AI, algorithms are used to process data, make decisions, and perform computations.

Artificial General Intelligence (AGI)

A type of AI that has the ability to understand, learn, and apply knowledge across a wide range of tasks, similar to human intelligence. AGI is also referred to as strong AI.

Artificial Intelligence (AI)

The simulation of human intelligence processes by machines, particularly computer systems. These processes include learning, reasoning, and self-correction.

Artificial Neural Network (ANN)

A computational model inspired by the human brain, consisting of interconnected nodes (neurons) that process information in layers. ANNs are used in machine learning and deep learning.

Autonomous Vehicle

A self-driving vehicle that uses AI and sensors to navigate and operate without human intervention. Autonomous vehicles rely on computer vision, machine learning, and other AI technologies.

B

Backpropagation

A supervised learning algorithm used for training neural networks. It involves calculating the gradient of the loss function with respect to each weight and updating the weights to minimize the loss.

Bayesian Network

A probabilistic graphical model that represents a set of variables and their conditional dependencies using a directed acyclic graph. Bayesian networks are used for reasoning and decision-making under uncertainty.

Big Data

Large and complex datasets that require advanced methods and technologies to store, process, and analyze. AI techniques, such as machine learning, are often used to extract insights from big data.

Bias

A systematic error in AI models that leads to unfair or inaccurate predictions. Bias can result from biased training data, algorithm design, or human influence. Addressing bias is crucial for ensuring fairness and accuracy in AI systems.

Black Box Model

An AI model whose internal workings are not easily interpretable or understood. Deep learning models, such as neural networks, are often considered black box models. Explainable AI aims to make these models more transparent.

C

Classification

A machine learning task that involves predicting the category or class label of a given input. Common classification algorithms include decision trees, support vector machines, and neural networks.

Clustering

An unsupervised learning task that involves grouping similar data points together based on their features. Common clustering algorithms include k-means, hierarchical clustering, and DBSCAN.

Computer Vision

A field of AI that enables machines to interpret and understand visual information from the world, such as images and videos. Applications of computer vision include image recognition, object detection, and facial recognition.

Convolutional Neural Network (CNN)

A type of neural network designed for processing structured grid data, such as images. CNNs use convolutional layers to capture spatial patterns and features. They are widely used in computer vision tasks.

Cross-Validation

A technique used to evaluate the performance of a machine learning model by partitioning the data into subsets, training the model on some subsets, and testing it on the remaining subsets. Cross-validation helps assess the model's generalizability.

D

Data Augmentation

A technique used to increase the diversity of a training dataset by creating modified versions of existing data. In image processing, data augmentation can include transformations like rotation, scaling, and flipping.

Data Mining

The process of discovering patterns, correlations, and insights from large datasets using statistical and computational techniques. Data mining is used in various fields, including marketing, finance, and healthcare.

Decision Tree

A machine learning algorithm that splits data into subsets based on feature values, creating a tree-like structure of decisions. Decision trees are used for classification and regression tasks.

Deep Learning

A subset of machine learning that involves neural networks with many layers (deep neural networks). Deep learning is used for complex tasks like image recognition, natural language processing, and speech recognition.

Dimensionality Reduction

A technique used to reduce the number of input features in a dataset while retaining the most important information. Common methods include Principal Component Analysis (PCA) and t-Distributed Stochastic Neighbor Embedding (t-SNE).

E

Epoch

One complete pass through the entire training dataset during the training process of a machine learning model. Multiple epochs are often used to improve the model's performance.

Ethics in AI

The study and application of moral principles and guidelines to ensure the responsible development and use of AI technologies. Ethical considerations include fairness, transparency, accountability, and the impact on society.

Explainable AI (XAI)

A subfield of AI focused on making AI models more transparent, interpretable, and understandable. XAI techniques aim to provide clear explanations for the decisions made by AI systems, enhancing trust and accountability.

Expert System

An AI system that uses a knowledge base of human expertise and inference rules to solve specific problems or make decisions. Expert systems are commonly used in domains like medical diagnosis and financial planning.

F

Feature Engineering

The process of selecting, transforming, and creating input features for a machine learning model. Effective feature engineering can improve model performance by providing relevant and meaningful data.

Feature Extraction

The process of identifying and extracting important features from raw data. In image processing, feature extraction techniques can include edge detection, texture analysis, and keypoint detection.

Federated Learning

A distributed machine learning approach that allows models to be trained across multiple decentralized devices or servers without sharing raw data. Federated learning enhances data privacy and security.

Fuzzy Logic

A form of logic that deals with reasoning and decision-making under uncertainty. Fuzzy logic allows for degrees of truth rather than binary true/false values, making it suitable for complex and ambiguous situations.

G

Generalization

The ability of a machine learning model to perform well on new, unseen data. A model that generalizes well can make accurate predictions on data outside of the training dataset.

Generative Adversarial Network (GAN)

A type of neural network architecture consisting of two

networks: a generator and a discriminator. The generator creates synthetic data, while the discriminator evaluates its authenticity. GANs are used for tasks like image generation and data augmentation.

Gradient Descent

An optimization algorithm used to minimize the loss function of a machine learning model by iteratively updating the model's parameters. Variants of gradient descent include stochastic gradient descent and mini-batch gradient descent.

Graph Neural Network (GNN)

A type of neural network designed to process data represented as graphs. GNNs are used in applications like social network analysis, molecular modeling, and recommendation systems.

H

Hyperparameter

A parameter that defines the structure or behavior of a machine learning model and is set before the training process. Examples of hyperparameters include learning rate, batch size, and the number of hidden layers in a neural network.

Hyperparameter Tuning

The process of selecting the optimal hyperparameters for a machine learning model. Techniques for hyperparameter tuning include grid search, random search, and Bayesian optimization.

Heuristic

A problem-solving approach that uses practical methods and shortcuts to find solutions that may not be optimal but are sufficient for the given context. Heuristics are often used in search algorithms and optimization problems.

Hidden Layer

A layer in a neural network that lies between the input and output layers. Hidden layers contain neurons that process and transform the input data, enabling the network to learn complex patterns.

I

Image Recognition

A computer vision task that involves identifying and classifying objects or features within an image. Image recognition applications include facial recognition, object detection, and medical imaging.

Inference

The process of making predictions or decisions based on a trained machine learning model. Inference involves applying the model to new, unseen data to obtain results.

Instance Segmentation

A computer vision task that involves segmenting an image

into individual objects and classifying each object separately. Instance segmentation combines object detection and semantic segmentation.

Internet of Things (IoT)

A network of interconnected devices that collect, exchange, and analyze data through sensors and communication technologies. AI is used in IoT applications to enable intelligent decision-making and automation.

J

Joint Probability Distribution

A probability distribution that represents the likelihood of multiple random variables occurring together. Joint probability distributions are used in probabilistic graphical models and Bayesian networks.

Jupyter Notebook

An open-source web application that allows users to create and share documents containing live code, equations, visualizations, and narrative text. Jupyter Notebooks are widely used in data science and AI for interactive analysis and experimentation.

K

K-Means Clustering

An unsupervised learning algorithm that partitions data into k clusters, where each data point belongs to the cluster with the nearest mean. K-means clustering is used for tasks like data segmentation and pattern recognition.

Kernel

A function used in machine learning algorithms, such as support vector machines, to transform data into a higher-dimensional space. Kernels enable the separation of data that is not linearly separable in the original space.

Knowledge Representation

The process of encoding information and relationships in a form that can be used by AI systems to reason and make decisions. Common methods include logical representations, semantic networks, and ontologies.

Knowledge Base

A collection of structured information and rules used by an expert system or AI application to solve problems and make decisions. Knowledge bases are built using domain-specific expertise and data.

L

Label

A tag or category assigned to a data point, used as the output in supervised learning tasks. Labels are used to train machine learning models to make predictions or classifications.

Latent Variable

A variable that is not directly observed but inferred from other observed variables. Latent variables are used in probabilistic models and factor analysis to represent hidden factors.

Learning Rate

A hyperparameter that determines the step size for updating the model's parameters during training. The learning rate controls how quickly the model converges to the optimal solution.

Logistic Regression

A supervised learning algorithm used for binary classification tasks. Logistic regression models the probability of an outcome as a function of input features using the logistic function.

M

Machine Learning

A subset of AI that focuses on developing algorithms and statistical models that enable computers to learn from and make predictions or decisions based on data. Machine learning includes supervised, unsupervised, and reinforcement learning.

Markov Decision Process (MDP)

A mathematical framework used to model decision-making problems where outcomes are partly random and partly under the control of a decision-maker. MDPs are used in reinforcement learning to represent environments.

Model

A representation of a system or process used to make predictions or decisions based on input data. In AI, models are trained on data to learn patterns and relationships.

Model Evaluation

The process of assessing the performance of a machine learning model using metrics such as accuracy, precision, recall, and F1 score. Model evaluation helps determine how well the model generalizes to new data.

N

Natural Language Processing (NLP)

A field of AI that focuses on the interaction between computers and human language. NLP involves tasks such as text analysis, language translation, sentiment analysis, and speech recognition.

Neural Network

A computational model inspired by the human brain, consisting of layers of interconnected nodes (neurons) that process information. Neural networks are used in machine learning and deep learning for tasks like image recognition and language processing.

Normalization

A preprocessing technique used to scale input features to a standard range, typically [0, 1] or [-1, 1]. Normalization improves the performance and convergence of machine learning models.

Null Hypothesis

A hypothesis used in statistical testing that assumes no effect or relationship between variables. The null hypothesis is tested against an alternative hypothesis to determine statistical significance.

O

Object Detection

A computer vision task that involves identifying and localizing objects within an image. Object detection algorithms output bounding boxes and class labels for detected objects.

Overfitting

A situation where a machine learning model learns the training data too well, including noise and outliers, resulting in poor generalization to new data. Techniques like regularization and cross-validation are used to prevent overfitting.

Optimization

The process of finding the best solution or parameter values for a given problem. In machine learning, optimization algorithms are used to minimize the loss function and improve model performance.

Outlier

A data point that differs significantly from other observations in the dataset. Outliers can affect the performance of machine learning models and may need to be identified and handled appropriately.

P

Principal Component Analysis (PCA)

A dimensionality reduction technique that transforms data into a lower-dimensional space while retaining the most important information. PCA identifies the principal components (directions of maximum variance) in the data.

Precision

A metric used to evaluate the performance of a classification model, defined as the ratio of true positive predictions to the total positive predictions. Precision measures the accuracy of positive predictions.

Predictive Analytics

The use of statistical and machine learning techniques to analyze historical data and make predictions about future events. Predictive analytics is used in fields like finance, healthcare, and marketing.

Preprocessing

The process of cleaning, transforming, and preparing data for analysis or training machine learning models. Preprocessing steps may include normalization, encoding, and handling missing values.

Q

Q-Learning

A model-free reinforcement learning algorithm that learns the value of taking a particular action in a particular state. Q-learning uses a Q-table to store and update the expected rewards for state-action pairs.

Quantum Machine Learning

A field that combines quantum computing and machine learning to develop algorithms that can solve complex problems more efficiently than classical algorithms. Quantum machine learning leverages the principles of quantum mechanics.

Query

A request for information or data from a database or information system. In AI, queries are used to retrieve relevant data for analysis or decision-making.

Queue

A data structure that follows the First-In-First-Out (FIFO) principle, where elements are added to the end and removed from the front. Queues are used in various algorithms and applications, including task scheduling and simulation.

R

Random Forest

An ensemble learning method that combines multiple decision trees to improve classification or regression performance. Random forests reduce overfitting and increase accuracy by averaging the predictions of individual trees.

Recurrent Neural Network (RNN)

A type of neural network designed for sequential data, where connections between neurons form directed cycles. RNNs are used for tasks like language modeling, speech recognition, and time series analysis.

Reinforcement Learning (RL)

A type of machine learning where an agent learns to make decisions by interacting with its environment and receiving rewards or penalties for its actions. The goal is to learn a policy that maximizes cumulative rewards.

Regularization

A technique used to prevent overfitting by adding constraints to the model. Common regularization methods include L1 (Lasso) and L2 (Ridge) regularization, which add penalty terms to the loss function.

S

Semi-Supervised Learning

A machine learning approach that combines labeled and unlabeled data for training. Semi-supervised learning is useful when labeled data is scarce but unlabeled data is abundant.

Semantic Segmentation

A computer vision task that involves assigning a class label to each pixel in an image, resulting in a detailed classification of different regions. Semantic segmentation is used in applications like autonomous driving and medical imaging.

Sentiment Analysis

A natural language processing task that involves determining the sentiment or emotion expressed in a text, such as positive, negative, or neutral. Sentiment analysis is used in social media monitoring, customer feedback analysis, and more.

Sequence-to-Sequence (Seq2Seq) Model

A neural network architecture used for tasks that involve mapping input sequences to output sequences, such as language translation and text summarization. Seq2Seq models typically use RNNs or Transformers.

Shapley Value

A concept from cooperative game theory used to distribute the total gains of a coalition among its players. In machine learning, Shapley values are used to explain the contributions of individual features to a model's predictions.

T

TensorFlow

An open-source machine learning framework developed by the Google Brain team. TensorFlow is widely used for building and training machine learning and deep learning models.

Transfer Learning

A machine learning technique where a pre-trained model is fine-tuned on a new, related task. Transfer learning leverages knowledge from the pre-trained model to improve performance on the target task.

Turing Test

A test proposed by Alan Turing to determine whether a machine can exhibit intelligent behavior indistinguishable from that of a human. A machine passes the Turing Test if a human evaluator cannot reliably distinguish between the machine and a human based on their responses.

Training Set

A dataset used to train a machine learning model. The training set contains input-output pairs that the model learns from to make predictions on new data.

U

Unsupervised Learning

A type of machine learning where the model is trained on unlabeled data, with the goal of finding hidden patterns or structures. Common unsupervised learning tasks include clustering and dimensionality reduction.

Underfitting

A situation where a machine learning model is too simple to capture the underlying patterns in the data, resulting in poor performance on both the training and testing data. Underfitting can be addressed by increasing the model complexity or using more relevant features.

Uncertainty Quantification

The process of quantifying the uncertainty in model predictions. Uncertainty quantification helps assess the confidence in predictions and identify areas where the model may need improvement.

Uniform Distribution

A probability distribution where all outcomes are equally likely. In a uniform distribution, each value within the specified range has the same probability of occurring.

V

Validation Set

A dataset used to tune the model's hyperparameters and evaluate its performance during training. The validation set helps prevent overfitting and ensures that the model generalizes well to new data.

Value Function

In reinforcement learning, a function that estimates the expected cumulative reward for a given state or state-action pair. Value functions are used to evaluate and improve the policy.

Variational Autoencoder (VAE)

A type of generative model that combines neural networks and variational inference to generate new data samples. VAEs are used for tasks like data augmentation and anomaly detection.

Vector Space Model

A mathematical model used to represent text documents as vectors in a multi-dimensional space. Vector space models are used in information retrieval and natural language processing to measure document similarity.

W

Weak AI

A type of AI designed to perform specific tasks or solve narrow problems. Weak AI, also known as narrow AI, does not possess general intelligence or the ability to perform a wide range of tasks.

Weight

A parameter in a neural network that is adjusted during training to minimize the loss function. Weights determine the strength of connections between neurons and influence the model's predictions.

Word Embedding

A dense vector representation of words that captures their semantic meanings and relationships. Common word embedding models include Word2Vec, GloVe, and FastText.

Wrapper Method

A feature selection technique that evaluates the performance of a machine learning model using different subsets of features. Wrapper methods help identify the most relevant features for improving model performance.

X

XGBoost

An open-source library that provides an efficient and scalable implementation of gradient boosting algorithms. XGBoost is widely used for regression, classification, and ranking tasks.

XML (eXtensible Markup Language)

A markup language used to encode documents and data

in a human-readable and machine-readable format. XML is commonly used for data exchange and representation in web services and applications.

XOR Problem

A classic problem in machine learning that involves classifying binary inputs based on their exclusive OR (XOR) relationship. The XOR problem is often used to demonstrate the limitations of linear classifiers and the capabilities of neural networks.

Explainability

The degree to which the internal workings and decisions of an AI model can be understood and interpreted by humans. Explainability is important for building trust and ensuring accountability in AI systems.

Y

Yield

In the context of AI and machine learning, yield refers to the output or results produced by a model or system. Yield can be measured in terms of accuracy, efficiency, or other performance metrics.

YOLO (You Only Look Once)

A real-time object detection model that predicts bounding boxes and class probabilities for objects in an image. YOLO is known for its speed and accuracy in detecting objects.

Yellowbrick

A Python library for visualizing the performance of machine learning models. Yellowbrick provides tools for visual diagnostics and evaluation, helping data scientists understand and improve their models.

Yelp Dataset

A publicly available dataset provided by Yelp for research and analysis. The Yelp Dataset contains information about businesses, reviews, and user interactions, and is commonly used for sentiment analysis and recommendation system research.

Z

Zero Shot Learning

A machine learning approach that enables models to recognize and classify objects they have never seen before. Zero shot learning relies on knowledge transfer and semantic relationships between known and unknown classes.

Z-Score

A statistical measure that quantifies the number of standard deviations a data point is from the mean of the dataset. Z-scores are used for outlier detection and standardizing data.

Zipf's Law

A principle that describes the frequency distribution of words in natural language. According to Zipf's Law, the frequency of a word is inversely proportional to its rank in the frequency table. This principle is used in natural language processing and information retrieval.

Z-Test

A statistical test used to determine whether there is a significant difference between the means of two populations. Z-tests are commonly used in hypothesis testing and inferential statistics.

Conclusion

This glossary provides definitions and explanations for key terms and concepts in AI, offering a valuable reference for learners and practitioners. As the field of AI continues to evolve, staying updated with the latest terminology and concepts is essential for understanding and navigating this dynamic landscape. Whether you are a beginner or an experienced professional, this glossary serves as a useful resource for enhancing your knowledge and expertise in AI.

CHAPTER 12: AI PROJECT WORKFLOW

Successfully implementing AI projects requires a systematic approach that encompasses various stages from initial ideation to deployment and maintenance. In this chapter, we will explore a comprehensive AI project workflow, detailing each step to ensure that your AI projects are well-planned, effectively executed, and continuously improved. The workflow includes problem definition, data collection and preparation, model selection, training and evaluation, deployment, and monitoring and maintenance.

Step 1: Problem Definition

Understanding the Business Problem

The first step in any AI project is to clearly define the problem you aim to solve. This involves understanding the business context, objectives, and constraints.

Key Questions to Address

- **What is the business objective?** Understand the primary goal, whether it is to increase revenue, reduce costs, improve customer satisfaction, etc.
- **Who are the stakeholders?** Identify the key stakeholders

and their roles in the project.

- **What are the expected outcomes?** Define the specific outcomes and metrics that will be used to measure the success of the project.

- **What are the constraints?** Consider the budget, timeline, resources, and any regulatory or ethical constraints.

Formulating the AI Problem

Once the business problem is understood, translate it into a specific AI problem.

Types of AI Problems

- **Classification**: Assigning categories to data points (e.g., spam detection, sentiment analysis).

- **Regression**: Predicting continuous values (e.g., house price prediction, sales forecasting).

- **Clustering**: Grouping similar data points (e.g., customer segmentation).

- **Recommendation**: Suggesting items to users based on their preferences (e.g., product recommendations).

- **Anomaly Detection**: Identifying unusual data points (e.g., fraud detection).

Defining Success Criteria

- **Performance Metrics**: Define the metrics that will be used to evaluate the model's performance (e.g., accuracy, precision, recall, F1 score, mean squared error).

- **Baseline Model**: Establish a baseline model or heuristic to compare the performance of the AI model.

Step 2: Data Collection and Preparation

Data Collection

Data is the foundation of any AI project. Collecting high-quality, relevant data is crucial for building effective AI models.

Sources of Data

- **Internal Data**: Data generated within the organization (e.g., sales records, customer interactions).

- **External Data**: Data obtained from external sources (e.g., public datasets, APIs, third-party providers).

- **Synthetic Data**: Data generated artificially using simulations or algorithms when real data is scarce or unavailable.

Data Acquisition Methods

- **APIs**: Using application programming interfaces to collect data from online sources.

- **Web Scraping**: Extracting data from websites using web scraping tools and libraries.

- **Manual Collection**: Gathering data manually through surveys, experiments, or manual entry.

Data Preparation

Raw data often requires cleaning and preprocessing before it can be used for model training.

Data Cleaning

- **Handling Missing Values**: Decide whether to fill missing values with imputation techniques or remove incomplete records.
- **Removing Duplicates**: Identify and remove duplicate records to ensure data quality.
- **Outlier Detection**: Detect and handle outliers that may skew the model's performance.

Data Transformation

- **Normalization and Scaling**: Normalize or scale numerical features to ensure they have similar ranges.
- **Encoding Categorical Variables**: Convert categorical variables into numerical format using techniques like one-hot encoding or label encoding.
- **Feature Engineering**: Create new features or transform existing ones to improve model performance.

Data Splitting

- **Training Set**: The portion of the data used to train the model.
- **Validation Set**: The portion of the data used to tune hyperparameters and evaluate the model during training.
- **Test Set**: The portion of the data used to assess the model's performance on unseen data.

Step 3: Model Selection

Choosing the Right Model

Selecting the appropriate model depends on the problem type, data characteristics, and performance requirements.

Model Categories

- **Linear Models**: Simple models such as linear regression and logistic regression, suitable for linearly separable data.
- **Decision Trees and Ensemble Methods**: Models like decision trees, random forests, and gradient boosting, suitable for capturing complex patterns and interactions.
- **Support Vector Machines (SVM)**: Effective for high-dimensional data and classification tasks.
- **Neural Networks**: Suitable for complex tasks such as image recognition, natural language processing, and time series forecasting.
- **Clustering Algorithms**: Algorithms like k-means and hierarchical clustering for grouping similar data points.

Model Evaluation Criteria

- **Performance Metrics**: Use appropriate metrics based on the problem type (e.g., accuracy, precision, recall, F1 score for classification; mean squared error for regression).
- **Computational Efficiency**: Consider the computational resources required for training and inference.
- **Interpretability**: Assess how easily the model's decisions can be understood and explained.
- **Scalability**: Evaluate the model's ability to handle large datasets and high-dimensional data.

Step 4: Model Training and Evaluation

Training the Model

Training the model involves optimizing its parameters to minimize the loss function and improve performance.

Hyperparameter Tuning

- **Grid Search**: Exhaustively searching through a predefined set of hyperparameters to find the best combination.
- **Random Search**: Randomly sampling hyperparameter combinations to find a good set.
- **Bayesian Optimization**: Using probabilistic models to guide the search for optimal hyperparameters.

Cross-Validation

- **K-Fold Cross-Validation**: Splitting the data into k subsets and training the model k times, each time using a different subset as the validation set.
- **Leave-One-Out Cross-Validation**: Using each data point as a validation set and training the model on the remaining data points.

Evaluating the Model

Evaluating the model's performance on the validation set helps assess its generalizability and identify potential issues.

Performance Metrics

- **Confusion Matrix**: A table that summarizes the performance of a classification model by showing the true positives, false positives, true negatives, and false negatives.

- **Precision and Recall**: Precision measures the accuracy of positive predictions, while recall measures the model's ability to identify all positive instances.

- **F1 Score**: The harmonic mean of precision and recall, providing a balanced evaluation of the model's performance.

- **ROC Curve and AUC**: The receiver operating characteristic curve and the area under the curve measure the model's ability to distinguish between classes.

Error Analysis

- **Identifying Misclassifications**: Analyzing misclassified instances to understand the model's weaknesses and areas for improvement.

- **Feature Importance**: Evaluating the importance of each feature in the model's predictions to identify key drivers and potential areas for feature engineering.

Step 5: Model Deployment

Preparing for Deployment

Deploying an AI model involves making it available for use in a production environment. This requires careful planning and consideration of various factors.

Deployment Options

- **Cloud-Based Deployment**: Hosting the model on cloud platforms such as AWS, Google Cloud, or Azure for scalability and ease of access.

- **On-Premises Deployment**: Deploying the model on local servers for better control and data privacy.

- **Edge Deployment**: Deploying the model on edge devices for real-time processing and low latency.

Model Packaging

- **Serialization**: Saving the trained model to a file format that can be easily loaded and used for inference (e.g., pickle, ONNX).

- **API Development**: Creating an API to enable communication between the model and other applications or systems (e.g., RESTful API, gRPC).

Deployment Process

- **Integration Testing**: Testing the model in a staging environment to ensure it integrates seamlessly with existing systems and workflows.

- **Continuous Integration and Deployment (CI/CD)**: Automating the deployment process to ensure quick and reliable updates to the model.

Monitoring and Maintenance

Monitoring and maintaining the deployed model is crucial for ensuring its ongoing performance and reliability.

Performance Monitoring

- **Real-Time Monitoring**: Tracking the model's performance in real-time to detect issues such as latency, errors, and performance degradation.

- **Periodic Evaluation**: Regularly evaluating the model's performance on new data to identify potential issues and areas for improvement.

Model Retraining

- **Drift Detection**: Identifying changes in the data distribution or target variable that may affect the model's performance.

- **Scheduled Retraining**: Periodically retraining the model with new data to ensure it remains accurate and relevant.

Maintenance and Updates

- **Bug Fixes**: Addressing any bugs or issues identified during monitoring.

- **Feature Updates**: Adding new features or improving existing ones based on user feedback and performance analysis.

Case Study: End-to-End AI Project

To illustrate the AI project workflow, let's consider a case study of an AI project for predicting customer churn in a telecommunications company.

Problem Definition

The company wants to reduce customer churn by predicting which customers are likely to leave. The business objective is to increase customer retention and reduce churn rates.

AI Problem

The AI problem is a binary classification task: predicting whether a customer will churn (yes/no) based on their usage patterns, demographic information, and service history.

Success Criteria

- **Performance Metrics**: Accuracy, precision, recall, and F1 score.
- **Baseline Model**: A simple heuristic based on historical churn rates.

Data Collection and Preparation

Data Collection

- **Internal Data**: Customer demographics, service usage, billing history, and customer support interactions.
- **External Data**: Market data and competitor information.

Data Preparation

- **Data Cleaning**: Handling missing values, removing duplicates, and addressing outliers.
- **Data Transformation**: Normalizing numerical features, encoding categorical variables, and creating new features such as average monthly usage and tenure.
- **Data Splitting**: Splitting the data into training (70%), validation (15%), and test (15%) sets.

Model Selection

The team considers several models, including logistic regression, decision trees, random forests, and gradient boosting.

Model Evaluation Criteria

- **Performance Metrics**: Precision, recall, F1 score.
- **Computational Efficiency**: The model should be efficient enough for real-time predictions.
- **Interpretability**: The model should provide insights into the factors driving churn.

Model Training and Evaluation

Training

- **Hyperparameter Tuning**: Using grid search to optimize hyperparameters for the random forest model.
- **Cross-Validation**: Performing k-fold cross-validation to ensure the model generalizes well.

Evaluation

- **Performance Metrics**: The random forest model achieves an accuracy of 85%, precision of 80%, recall of 75%, and F1 score of 77%.
- **Error Analysis**: Identifying misclassifications and evaluating feature importance to refine the model.

Model Deployment

Deployment Preparation

- **Cloud-Based Deployment**: Hosting the model on AWS for scalability.
- **API Development**: Creating a RESTful API to enable communication between the model and the company's CRM system.

Deployment Process

- **Integration Testing**: Ensuring the model integrates seamlessly with the CRM system.
- **CI/CD**: Automating the deployment process using Jenkins.

Monitoring and Maintenance

Performance Monitoring

- **Real-Time Monitoring**: Using AWS CloudWatch to monitor the model's performance and detect issues.
- **Periodic Evaluation**: Evaluating the model's performance on new data every month.

Model Retraining

- **Drift Detection**: Monitoring for changes in data distribution and retraining the model as needed.
- **Scheduled Retraining**: Retraining the model with new data every six months.

Maintenance and Updates

- **Bug Fixes**: Addressing any issues identified during monitoring.

- **Feature Updates**: Adding new features based on customer feedback and performance analysis.

Conclusion

Implementing an AI project requires a structured and systematic approach that encompasses problem definition, data collection and preparation, model selection, training and evaluation, deployment, and monitoring and maintenance. By following this comprehensive AI project workflow, you can ensure that your AI projects are well-planned, effectively executed, and continuously improved. This approach not only enhances the likelihood of project success but also ensures that the AI solutions developed are reliable, scalable, and impactful.

www.ingramcontent.com/pod-product-compliance
Lightning Source LLC
Chambersburg PA
CBHW071457220526
45472CB00003B/833